Typing: A life in 26 keys

"*Typing: A Life in Twenty-Six Keys* is a complex and fascinating book.... At moments it is as funny as Cohen could be.... In this winning and brave memoir he tries to figure out what he is as a writer and what his place is in his own country and in the world."
The Gazette

"Written in a direct conversational manner, filled with personal reflections, replete with anecdotes and vivid portraits, this affecting and honest work that covers three decades of Canadian cultural life should find an appreciative reading audience."
The Hamilton Spectator

"*Typing*...offer[s] some brilliant, telling snapshots of people who crossed Cohen's path, including [Margaret] Laurence, and such other literary heavyweights as Margaret Atwood, Morley Callaghan, Hugh Garner, Anna Porter, Robert Fulford and Jack McClelland." *Ottawa Citizen*

"The late Matt Cohen paints a picture of himself as a man who spent most of his adult life as a 'struggling writer.' Cohen was a craftsman, a man who wanted to say things that were important, moving, exciting, funny, memorable.... Immensely moving, the story of a man who spent his life using words." *The Chronicle– Herald* (Halifax)

"*Typing: A Life in 26 Keys* is important not only for what it reveals about one of the country's most respected writers, but for the light it sheds on the years during which Canadian culture came of age. *Typing: A Life in 26 Keys* remains a deeply affecting work, an eloquent conclusion to a life devoted to writing." *The Record* (Kitchener-Waterloo)

Typing

A life in
26 keys

Matt Cohen

Vintage Canada

A Division of Random House of Canada Limited

VINTAGE CANADA EDITION, 2001

Published in Canada by Vintage Canada, a division of
Random House of Canada Limited, in 2001. First published in hardcover
in Canada by Random House Canada, Toronto, in 2000. Distributed by
Random House of Canada Limited, Toronto.

Vintage Canada and colophon are registered trademarks of
Random House of Canada Limited.

Some of this material appeared in different forms in
Toronto Life and *Books in Canada*.

National Library of Canada Cataloguing in Publication Data

Cohen, Matt, 1942–1999
Typing : a life in twenty-six keys

Includes index.
ISBN 0-679-31124-6

1. Cohen, Matt, 1942–1999. 2. Authors, Canadian—
20TH century—Biography. I. Title.

PS8555.04Z53 2001   C813'.54   C2001-900861-9
PR9199.3.C58Z475 2001

www.randomhouse.ca

Printed and bound in the United States of America

2 4 6 8 9 7 5 3 1

Anyone who knew Matt will notice that many important people and events in his life cannot be found in this book. They will also know how rich and complex his nonwriting life was.

Matt wrote *Typing* in five months after he was diagnosed with lung cancer and finished three weeks before he died. It is about what led him to be a writer and what shaped the books he wrote over his long and prolific career.

—Patsy Aldana

Contents

Child,

Father,

Literature

----

how literature becomes the escape
from a crazed rootless past where
everything is hypocritical

Jew is a person in exile from nowhere.
Or maybe that's a myth I like to believe because the truth is too oppressive.

Born into a religion strong on primogeniture, I was the first male grandchild on either side of my family. All four of my grandparents were, each in their own way, uncomfortable remnants of Russian-Jewish life in the nineteenth century, and my parents hastily rejected what they took to be their own parents' crazed immigrant mentality in order to assimilate into their idealistic version of the North American dream, Canadian variation.

By the time I was born, on December 30, 1942, my parents had established themselves in Kingston, Ontario. My father, a chemist, had a job at the now defunct Monarch Battery Company. With the perverse pride that accompanied all such stories, he explained to me that this job was the only one he was offered in a year of searching after he received his doctorate, the reason for the difficulty being that he was Jewish. The moral of the

story was, of course, that a Jew—and this went double
for a Jew named Cohen—had to be better than everyone else because the deck would always be stacked
against him. This same moral served many of his remi-
niscences, and it went along with his cheerful motto:
"When you're a Cohen, you have to believe your shit
smells better."

When my mother was six months pregnant with me,
she developed acute appendicitis. The doctor, forced to
choose between an unborn fetus and a twenty-five-year-
old woman, selected the latter. This was either the first
time someone tried to kill me or my first drug experience.
When my mother had recovered from the operation she
celebrated by falling down the basement stairs.

My godmother was a pianist, a Parisian Jew who escaped France on the last boat allowed free passage before
the German invasion. The ship had Jews on the upper
decks, the French treasury stashed below. Stopped by a
U-boat off the English coast, the captain declared there
was "no cargo of interest" and the ship was allowed to
proceed to Montreal.

Every day after my birth my godmother and my family
doctor came to visit me. My godmother sang me songs
while the doctor waved his gold pocket watch in front of
my eyes. My mother thought they were doing some kind
of early musical training until the doctor admitted he was
testing for brain damage. When it became clear that I
would survive being born, I began bringing up everything
I was fed and was on the point of starvation when someone thought of giving me goat's milk. That I could digest,
and apparently it gave me the strength to spend the nights

having colic attacks. In sum, I was one of those babies who got off to an eventful beginning.

All four of my grandparents had fled from what it meant to be a Jew in Russia at the beginning of this century—on the surface, pogroms, below the surface more elaborate versions of the same. Via New York and Montreal they settled in Western Canada and started having children. The children eagerly planned to escape their immigrant parents in order to live the life of enlightened North American Jews who had put the Old World behind them in order to better embrace the New.

For my father this ideal was Enlightenment Man as described by Isaiah Berlin: an atheist, a rationalist, a believer in knowledge as virtue, a person convinced that the world is a giant jigsaw puzzle of which we've seen only discordant pieces, but which a being of perfect intelligence and knowledge could fit together.

My mother was willing to play along with all this though she had no interest in the details. Her attraction was to mainstream European and North American culture, from French Impressionist painting to existentialism; from classical music to ballet and Shakespearean theatre; from New York musicals to American novels and magazines such as *The Atlantic Monthly*, *The Reporter*, *The New Yorker*, etc.

Neither of them was taking on anything totally inconsistent with their past, but the centre of gravity had obviously shifted. They hadn't "rejected" their Jewishness. They were synagogue members, most of their friends were Jewish and they were adamantly in favour—at least until the time came—of their two sons dating and marrying Jewish girls. On the other hand, the cultural and geographic gap between them and their parents was hardly coincidental. In marrying each other they had, much more than their siblings, made a perhaps unspoken pact to tear themselves away from their parents and their parents' kind of life.

On their arrival from the Russian Pale after the pogroms of 1905, my mother's parents and many of their relatives established themselves in Winnipeg. My grandfather eventually got a job at the Ford assembly plant, where he stayed until it closed in the 1930s. He then moved to Toronto—this too was a move made by many relatives and friends—in search of work. For the first year my mother, who would have liked to go to university, stayed behind and worked as a secretary so that the family, which included her two younger siblings and my grandmother's somewhat demented father, would have at least one sure source of income.

My grandfather eventually opened a garage in Toronto; it staggered along until his death, when my uncle took it over and (much to my father's disgust) sacrificed all his other plans to rescue my grandfather's name by paying off his debts and proving that the business could be run successfully. Religiously observant more out of habit than conviction, my maternal grandparents were freethinking Zionists who seemed much more concerned with enjoying and surviving the present than worrying about details of religious dogma.

Of all my grandparents the one I most admired as a child was my maternal grandfather. He had studied the violin in his youth and could still play sweet rhythmic tunes on an old instrument that he kept wrapped in a soft velvety cloth. When it seemed that I learned quickly he actually gave me the violin, and I took lessons for several years. I had inherited the ability to make my fingers jump around quickly but not his sense of pitch. I still have the violin. Aside from a few prayer books I don't understand, it is the only physical object I possess that belonged to any of my grandparents. Whenever I pick it up I am reminded of him and how I saw him when I was a child: he seemed entirely low-key, free of stress, and devoted to the moment (later I realized this impression was an illusion). Despite his abilities with the violin, I thought his most amazing trick was standing on his head, a position he could attain in several different and unlikely ways. He taught me the easiest ones, but though I can still get myself upside down, it has never had the effect on my children or nieces that it had on me. He also used to let me prowl around his garage, an oily disorganized repository of various items that one day might come in useful. He had a penchant for investing in things like longer-lasting oil filters and amazing sewing machines.

When my grandfather died I was only eleven years old, and I was completely devastated. My grandmother came to live with us in Ottawa for a while. She had fallen into a long depression for which her therapy seemed to be making fish-shaped pottery ashtrays. Eventually she cured herself by moving back to Toronto to live near her other relatives and friends, and when I eventually moved to Toronto I visited her. The woman she'd become seemed unconnected to the woman she'd been in the joyous household I knew as a child, and though I should have found this lesson in loss and aging a valuable one, my visits were infrequent.

My other grandfather was a deeply religious man who studied Torah his whole life. If my mother's father's familiar territory was the gasoline-soaked disorder of his garage and the iron-and-steel mysteries of the automobile engine, that of my father's father was the Orthodox synagogue, with its serene atmosphere of God-decreed orderly eternity, its wooden benches polished by the trousers of the faithful, its curtained-off area for the women, its bimah and its Torah.

Short, stocky, of legendary strength, he always wore a large yarmulke, which partially hid the fact that he had lost all his hair at twenty-five after a bout of scarlet fever— though to me, his large muscular skull was even more impressive than a full head of hair would have been. In the story "Racial Memories" I borrowed my grandfather for my narrator and described the almost other-worldly way I saw him: ". . . the hats he wore outside had brims which kept the sun away and left the skin of his face a soft and strangely attractive waxy white. White, too, were his square-fingered hands, the moons of his nails, his squarish slightly-gapped teeth, the carefully washed and ironed shirts my grandmother supplied for his thrice-daily trips to synagogue. A typical sartorial moment: on the day before his seventieth birthday I found him outside on a kitchen stepladder wearing slippers but no socks, his suit pants held up by suspenders, his white shirt complete with what we used to call bicep-pinchers, his outdoors hat—

decked out in style, in other words, even though he was sweating rivers while he trimmed the branches of his backyard cherry tree."

My grandfather had trained to be a rabbi, and he was always active in the Orthodox religious community though, after his arrival in Canada, he became a businessman, a junk dealer specializing in scrap metal. As a parent he was strict and demanding. The actual discipline was left to my grandmother, whose personality made her more suited to the meting out of punishment. Of the couple it seemed my grandfather was the affectionate one, yet lost in a world of prayer and ritual that seemed to have no connection with the world I inhabited.

My grandmother, a handsome and intelligent woman, was always threatening to expire from acute digestive problems. She married my grandfather when she was only sixteen—this was in order to legally travel with him to Canada in the same wave of emigration that brought my mother's parents. Her family were market gardeners, but also part of the self-declared aristocracy of her village. Although as a woman she could not have the formal education my grandfather had received, she displayed a certain intellectual flash, which unfortunately was accompanied by such total doctrinal rigidity that eventually everyone found it easier to lie to her. This meant, in the end, that one of her granddaughters married a non-Jew and had children while my grandmother kept asking her why she hadn't yet met a nice boy.

My relations with her were even worse. When my parents told her I was marrying a non-Jew, she decided, supposedly on behalf of my dead grandfather, to declare me dead and go into mourning. Normally she would not have been informed: but my father, on what he thought to be his deathbed, though it wasn't, had decided to use the occasion to stop lying to her. By this time in her life she always wore a black dress so I doubt that the effort and additional grief involved in mourning for me were too much of a burden. Actually I admired her capacity for fanatic stubbornness; I considered the whole thing a necessary comic drama, which I didn't hold against her. That intractable will was a trait she had passed on to my father, and I sometimes suspect he passed it on to me. When my son Daniel was born (by this point I was living with Patsy Aldana, a non-Jew to whom I was not married) my grandmother was ninety-two years old. She was trapped in a hospital bed in North Toronto and most people were still telling her the lies she wanted to hear. For example, when my father died no one dared tell her though she kept asking why he had stopped writing her letters. Nonetheless she somehow found out about Daniel and made it known she wanted to see him.

The visit was arranged: mother, child and my mother went to see her. All went smoothly. I refused to accompany them on the grounds that having been declared dead once I intended to stay that way.

My father was of medium height, had a wide face with a frankly large nose, big ears, a wide mobile mouth always ready to scowl, grin or settle into a frown of concentration, blue eyes behind the thick lenses of his horn-rimmed glasses, sparse straight hair always parted to one side, strong sloping shoulders and long powerful arms developed in the family junkyard, a slight paunch, a stoop, skinny white hairless legs, leather slippers with a cutting-edge odour that justified his habit of changing his socks every day when he came home from work, a long-legged stride he claimed to have developed walking across the prairies to school, and an aggressive way of pushing his head forward when he wanted to make a point. Kindly but with a temper, emotionally direct, my father was the prototypical 1950s male rock on which our family—my mother, my brother and I—depended.

He liked to talk about his own childhood, which he portrayed as a vividly coloured Hell governed by tyrannical parents descended straight from the Middle Ages, his insufferably brilliant and handsome gold-medal-winning older brother, his horribly bossy older sister and his unjustly spoiled little brother. (Eventually I would get to know all of these siblings—each had his or her charm, each was also terrified by their parents, and each saw my father as fearsomely single-minded and stubborn.)

Of course the escape from this Hell had to be mythic, and it was: summoning his entire and enormous brainpower, my father skipped several grades during which other mere mortals spent years learning things he figured out for himself on his way to Hebrew school. He both entered and graduated from Brandon College at unbelievably early ages, and after capturing all the prizes Brandon had to offer he won a scholarship to the University of Toronto. Carrying an eighth-hand suitcase he climbed into a freezing cattle car in the mid-1930s to make his triumphant journey east to join his brother, who was already rewriting the cosmos at U of T.

In the years before he made his escape my father put in long afternoons and holidays working in my grandfather's scrap metal yard. Splitting batteries was the task he talked about. We were invited to imagine him, a tiny child, having to earn his supper by swinging a huge sledge into a car battery in order to access its valuable copper innards.

After the cattle-car escape, he did no more physical labour. By the time I was ten years old my mother would plead with me to mow the lawn to spare my father the inevitable heart attack such activity would cause a man of his age. In any case he was too busy playing tennis and golf to have time for the lawn.

The year I discovered war comics, I had to consider the fact that my father hadn't gone to war. He *had* been a scientist who helped with the war effort, first making batteries for tanks, then doing work for the heavy water plant in Chalk River (a job that may have had very direct consequences for my own health). In any case, he had flat feet and was legally blind. But his lack of military status was still vaguely embarrassing. Other families on the block had framed pictures of fathers in uniform. It made me wonder how my father had coped with people thinking that somehow he had gotten off easily, or maybe even thinking it himself. It was easy to feel my father had "gotten off." He was a research scientist, a government employee at the time when the motto of the civil service was "once hired, never fired." The other men on the street were a washing machine salesman, an insurance man, a violin teacher, a furniture store owner, a car salesman and a lawyer. Their jobs, their livelihoods, were constantly at risk. In many of the houses there was a feeling that life had cut too close to the bone. My father, no richer, had a future as sure as eternity. Or so it seemed to me.

There were two other Jewish families on the street, one in the house across from us and one next door. We were a little Christmas-tree-free zone with inhabitants who hid discreetly on religious holidays and tried to stay invisible on Sundays. On Saturdays, my brother and I would leave the house in suits and yarmulkes to go to the synagogue. The other kids would be riding bikes, shooting each other with water pistols, organizing football games. In my bar mitzvah year, as we walked by, I would be carrying a velvet bag containing talliths and tefillin, and they would look at us as though we had leprosy. On the way home it was a different story. They knew we were only minutes away from reappearing in jeans and as we went by we would be assigned teams. Other times, though never when I was dressed up, they would shout "Jew" and "kike." I sometimes ran, but eventually ended up standing and fighting because between cowboy movies and hearing about concentration camps and the Warsaw Ghetto, I'd been forced to realize that the only ending was a violent one.

One afternoon, I fought a boy who'd been shouting anti-Semitic junk at my brother on the Fisher Park skating rink. It was a Saturday afternoon. My father had taken us to the rink and had left us there to amuse ourselves skating in circles. The idea was that this would give us a valuable opportunity to exhaust ourselves with exercise and fresh air while my mother got some time alone and my father hid out somewhere doing errands.

When my father arrived to collect us at the end of the afternoon he found us in exile on the children's rink. We'd been barred from the main rink because I'd hit a boy who'd been yelling "chicken Jew" every time my brother skated past. Instead of being proud of me, he took us home without comment. For a long time I pondered the meaning of his reaction, but in the end I gave up. What I remembered instead was the soggy feeling of trying to manoeuvre on my skates and box at the same time, and the even more unlikely sensation of my mittened fist crunching into someone's face.

One day when I was about sixteen my father, perhaps in a confessional mood, told me that he ate bacon in restaurants when he was away for conferences. This was announced with total gravity, as though he were informing me that he was having an affair with a princess from a minor principality.

"Oh," I said. "Do you have the bacon with eggs?"

"Or in sandwiches," he said. "But I don't like ham."

"What about butter?" I asked. In our home we had only margarine—that way we wouldn't mix dairy with meat. In my father's father's house, such false coin was not permitted: with meat meals he garnished his bread with salt.

"No butter," my father said. "Sometimes a glass of milk."

It developed that as a scientist and a rational human being, he had decided to be an atheist. In order to avoid hurting his parents' feelings he had never informed them of this decision—in fact, so far as they knew he went to synagogue every week. He didn't, but he had forced my brother and me to go to synagogue and have bar mitzvahs. He had even attempted, unsuccessfully, to keep us going after our bar mitzvahs. He had always pretended to us that he was a believer.

"I'd appreciate if you didn't say anything about this to my parents," was how my father concluded his confession. The reason he was telling me this now was that in a year I would be going to the University of Toronto to study Maths, Physics and Chemistry, and I would be expected to dine with his parents every Friday night, and uphold the series of pretences he had established to keep his "good son" status intact.

Of course, I could have upbraided my father for his hypocrisy. On the other hand, I had my own hidden agenda: the truth was that I was not on my way to U of T to study science because I wanted to be a scientist. I wouldn't have minded discovering the theory of relativity or even a comet if I could do it in five minutes, but the idea of actually going to work every day, in a laboratory or anywhere else, was out of the question. I was going to study science for two reasons: first because it might get me my father's approval—I desperately craved it and nothing else had ever worked. Second, because I could leave Ottawa and go to the University of Toronto, known in our household as the Mecca of science because my father had earned his doctorate there. If I studied arts, and of course he would not for the world try to influence my decision—even though everyone knew the study of arts was reserved for those whose brains and psyches were too feeble to tear off the blinders of superstition and ignorance, get out their slide rules and figure out how the universe worked—I might as well save money by staying at home and going to Carleton, a university whose scientific facilities were deemed so second-rate by my father that he always bowed his head when speaking of them.

When it became clear that due to falling standards and grade inflation I would actually be accepted into the University of Toronto, my father took me there to meet some of his old friends in the chemistry department.

It was the spring of my final year of high school. I had grown bored with my courses and almost completely detached from the school. At that time 100 per cent of the final marks were decided by provincially set exams marked in Toronto, so there was no reason to attend classes. The U of T campus, with its Gothic stone buildings, its lawns and its trees, its enormous library, looked like a paradise.

Aside from the fact that I couldn't imagine going to work every day the actual stuff of science was impenetrable to me. By high school standards I was good at math, and in fact the same skill would allow me to coast through university. But with mathematics, you're either a genius or a no one. I knew I was in the latter category.

Of course, not every scientist is a great mathematician. Attention to detail, acute powers of observation and meticulous work habits are equally essential. My father's friends, for example, were all engaged in directing experiments that involved enormously complex charts and graphs. I knew this was not something I could get involved in. Making a chart, for me, had always been a good excuse to spill the whole bottle of ink on the page. Detail? Meticulous observation? Alas, I already knew myself to be more in-clined to facile rhetoric and making things up.

During my first couple of months in Maths, Physics and Chemistry, I missed most of my lectures because I was so excited to be away from home I stayed up nights read-ing and then slept through most of the day. The only courses that interested me were English, calculus and phi-losophy. Physics, chemistry and numerical analysis were as indigestible and foreign to me as the arcane religious dogmas I'd been exposed to in my Hebrew school days. I decided to switch into the arts.

Calling or writing my father to ask him about switch-ing directions was not a strategy that appealed. That left doing the deed and presenting it as a *fait accompli*. I was, however, required to get signed permission from two professors. My English professor was a don in my resi-dence and quickly agreed. The other signature I needed was from my philosophy professor, Marcus Long. Profes-sor Long, then approaching retirement, had enjoyed a long and illustrious career at the University of Toronto. Author of the standard first-year text on philosophy and a popular public lecturer, he was an old-fashioned liberal-humanist devoted to grave discussions of "values," and infamous for his parallel fidelity to various libations—a fidelity that by this time had made its mark on his physical presence.

After several attempts (it was nearing Christmas break) I found him in his office, a picturesque book-lined den in a corner of University College, slumped over with his head resting on his desk. I stood silent for a few moments, hoping he would wake up, then gave a few discreet coughs.

When this didn't work, I sat down opposite his desk and began talking about my last essay as though we were in the middle of a conversation. After a couple of minutes he woke up and began shaking his head back and forth like a large dog suddenly caught in the rain.

I explained to him that due to the stimulating and revelatory effect of his classes and his book I had decided to give up science and pursue the humanities. When he didn't reply, I put the form that needed signing in front of him. He seemed on the verge of passing out again, but suddenly mustered himself enough to scrawl his name and ask, "Who are you?" I told him my name, took the form and left. As I went out the door he gave a great sigh and once more lowered his head.

Early in the spring term my father made an unannounced trip to Toronto. Sitting on my chair looking at my bookcase, he noticed (being a scientist he did have strong powers of observation) that I had a lot of texts for courses such as English, philosophy, political science and economics, but none for physics and chemistry. The ensuing conversation was unpleasant and for the next several years we hardly spoke.

Although my father had often made it clear that no male who was not a real scientist could be considered a real person, his view of the arts was mysterious to me. Our home, with its full complement of literature, art and music, had always appeared devoted to the arts. My mother played the piano, my father sometimes sang in the synagogue choir, there were sculptures and prints of famous paintings. But most of all there were books; one of my very first memories is of bookcases. I must have been about three years old. I am incredibly short, the ceiling is incredibly high and I am walking towards an enormous set of bookcases. They rise, tall and massive icons filled with rows of weird vertical boxes packed side by side.

I remember standing there, suitably dazzled by this household monument that rose from the very ground under my feet towards the sky—and with this memory comes the feeling of my jaw dropping as I gaze upwards like one of the awestruck primates in *2001: A Space Odyssey*. Books, it seemed, were the household gods. No one needed to tell me that. They had their altars, and they were worshipped by parents, and eventually children, on a daily basis.

In the evenings my father was always to be found slumped in his armchair reading. He was a scientist ("a real scientist," as he always reminded us) but he read books in every field because in his opinion it was not acceptable to know less than everything.

My mother also read—various works in psychology first for her part-time studies at the university and later for her job as a social worker with a caseload of "underprivileged" children, but most enthusiastically a steady stream of fiction: novels and short story collections both American and Canadian, as well as the stories in the various magazines that made their way into our house.

My brother and I caught the habit. I suppose my parents read for escape, for edification, for amusement. I read to find out what adults were doing (American writers were great for this purpose) and also because once I had a book in my head, everything else disappeared, most notably my anxieties about school and undone homework. Fiction drew me in hypnotically; anything I started, I had to finish. Now that I myself write fiction, reading has become a complex amalgam of escape, research and professional curiosity. Only occasionally does a book capture me the way it used to. In those days I was absolutely open to the printed word, the devoted slave of any novel that could keep my attention through the first page.

One night when I was a teenager, I found on the living-room coffee table a book called *Under the Ribs of Death*, by John Marlyn. I had never heard of the title or the author. Looking at the flap copy I saw it had been written by a Canadian and was an account of growing up on the Prairies before the Second World War. This struck me as a peculiar subject, but I nonetheless took it up to my room, put it between the pages of my history text, and began to read.

By the time I had finished the book, with a couple of detours for essential homework, it was well after midnight. I went downstairs in search of a snack. The lights were still on: my father was ensconced in his armchair, his slippered feet extended on his stool, reading a mystery.

It should be said that there was a distinct change in our house as midnight approached. By eleven-thirty or so, the official day and all the rules that went with it, were over. It was the hour when my father settled in to read mysteries and science fiction books, an indulgence that put him into an indulgent mood. At ten o'clock my descent into the living room was guaranteed to bring questions about the state of my homework, but a similar appearance at midnight was either ignored or greeted with a benign nod. If my mother was awake she would be in a housecoat, making hot chocolate or preparing to watch a late movie. My own appearances were always forays for books or food, and I was encouraged to consume both in unlimited quantities.

But on this night when I put the John Marlyn book back on the coffee table, my father turned his own book upside down and looked at me curiously. "So?" he asked.

He'd never shown any interest in my reaction to other books so it took me a moment to realize he wanted to know what I thought of this one.

"Okay, I guess," I said. The description of the bleakness of life during the Depression hadn't particularly moved me. I'd already gotten the general idea from him and my mother; they were both given to complaining about the rigours of life in the thirties, and I suppose I had been hoping for a comic parody of all that, or maybe something with a political edge, like the John Steinbeck novels I'd read. On the other hand, I'd read it from beginning to end, grateful for the escape.

"Not bad," I said to my father.

"Hmph," my father said, in that sceptical way he had. "Do you know it took him years to write that book?"

I thought my father must have read an article on the author somewhere.

"He worked on it all the time. His wife had to have a job."

"Mom has a job," I said. Although it was rare for women to work at that time it certainly wasn't unknown, and I suppose because many of my teachers were women, and my own mother worked, I didn't see this activity as being abnormal.

"She *had* to work," my father said. He stood, picking up the Marlyn book in his big hands. He was a calm man, my father, but also stubborn and single-minded, and he had a temper that sparked somewhere deep inside him, then rose slowly to the surface. "You really think this is what life was like then?"

"I wasn't there," I said, wondering if he was actually going to tear the book to pieces.

"There's no joy here," my father said, "nothing but bitterness."

Later I would realize that he felt John Marlyn was using the false front of literature to pass judgement on him, or if not him, personally, then those he had known, the web of life that had been his. But at that moment I saw only the other side, my father taking a book, subtracting it from the world of literature and assessing its potential as personal insult.

"He spent seven years writing *this*," my father said angrily, "and there's nothing in it."

He set the book down. "I used to write plays in university," he said. "Then I grew up."

He had destroyed something in himself (or someone had) with such savagery that he couldn't help wanting to inflict the same wound on me. Nonetheless, he hadn't meant to let himself go, and as always after he lost his temper, he turned away.

On December 30, 1963, I turned twenty-one. I was in fourth year, my last year of undergraduate studies in political economy, and had absolutely no idea what I would do if I ever grew up. As a combined birthday-graduation present, which was also a peace offering after the frosty period that had followed my switching courses, my father gave me a green portable Olivetti typewriter.

I had always believed my life would begin at twenty-one—everything else was mere prelude to this moment. I expected that the years from twenty-one to twenty-five, when old age was scheduled to set in, would be an eternity of perfection. So far, everything was on schedule. As my birthday approached it seemed to me I was entering into my prime. At five foot eight, I was rapidly approaching my full height. I was skinny, full of aimless energy, finally coming into something that, if not happiness, was an emotional universe I was happy to live in.

At the beginning of January 1964 I took my typewriter back to Toronto to begin this real life, life at twenty-one, of which I had been so certain. On the day of my return I saw a poster announcing a fiction contest at University College, my college, with a prize large enough to finance a summer trip to Europe. For years I'd been writing stories and sending them *to The New Yorker, The Atlantic Monthly* and, once, *Seventeen*. They'd always come back, though *Seventeen* had liked my story so much that a sympathetic editor had taped a Canadian quarter to the rejection letter to repay my postage.

But now I was twenty-one. Everything would be different, including the worldly success of my fiction.

I was living at 55 Harbord Street, a dilapidated Victorian mansion known as Peace House because it was inhabited by students who, like me, considered themselves part of the radical student left, informally known as "the movement"—*movement* being used to distinguish its spontaneous participatory democracy from the top-down organization of political parties.

Writing short stories was not exactly what revolutionaries were supposed to be doing. Nor was deserting the cause to go to Europe and live in a garret. But despite its name, Peace House was not exactly a Dostoyevskian cell of dedicated politicos. Like the others who lived there I had volunteered to pay my share of the rent, and I didn't mind the sound of the mimeograph machines grinding out pamphlets late into the night. Where the growing swell of political activity might lead, no one knew. In 1964 no one in Toronto could know that the fifties were about to mutate into the sixties, yet the Kennedy assassination, the Cuban missile crisis and the civil rights movement in the United States had all announced that what had seemed solid ground was turning queasy. The postwar certainties were dissolving and a door was opening to an unknowable future for which we had vague but utopian hopes (though cynics like myself tended to suspect that the glorious unknowable future might, like so many other such futures, bear a distinct resemblance to various disastrous pasts).

In January of 1964, I set up my new typewriter and a stack of blank paper. Although my literary ambitions had some long-standing roots, there was also another factor: I had a crush on a certain blonde English major who had told me, after reading one of my juvenile efforts—the heart-rending story of a young man walking in the rain and pining after a certain "Maria" whose name echoed evocatively to the rhythm of his sodden feet on the pavement, etc.—that she thought I "had talent." She was also planning to go to Europe, on the very trip for which I was planning to buy a ticket with my winning entry to the contest.

She was—I considered—a beatnik. She had long stringy hair, wore sandals, drank wine and, most telling of all, ate olives. When I presented her with the magnificent news of my new goal, she advised me to enhance my writing persona by dressing in baggy corduroys in order to look like Ernest Hemingway. Ernest Hemingway? I was a bit puzzled by her choice. I would have expected Jean-Paul Sartre or James Joyce. Like them I was extremely myopic; surely the rest would follow. But Ernest Hemingway? Did she see me tramping around on safaris? Growing a beard and getting her to call me Papa? I had read some of Hemingway's books as a teenager and taken away the impression of an intolerant anti-Semite, a man's man full of ridiculous illusions about himself, a boasting buffoon. I had, however, read his books from cover to cover and now, when I looked at his stories again and set them beside Joyce's *Dubliners*, I saw in them something else: an undeniable urge to penetrate to the core of his own obsessions, however twisted, with death and sex. I also had to consider that he was a man who had achieved world fame and made a lot of money from his writing. And finally, when I ignored the actual meaning of his sentences, I had to admire the way they were put together. So I bought a cheap pair of corduroys of a deep velvety brown and began to wear them as I typed and retyped my contest masterpieces.

When summer arrived, I was still wearing the corduroys, by now a stained and faded beige with a smooth seat on the verge of splitting. I had won the fiction contest and was living in a barn not far from the Paris suburb of Sarcelles. The blonde had married a fiancé I hadn't known about. I was officially a sculptor's assistant plastering the inside wall of a huge barn so he could use it as the background for constructing a welded-metal mosaic commissioned by a rich American for his swimming pool. Despite the clothes, my Hemingway phase was over. More erratic mentors had gained my attention. I was now writing first-person Henry Miller-type prose (without the sex), and a long poem in imitation of T.S. Eliot. My diet consisted of tomatoes, eggs, baguettes and free drinks supplied at the local tavern by old First World War soldiers paying tribute to the fact I was a Canadian.

In theory, nothing could be more portentous than spending the summer Carnaby Street exploded in France, pretending to be an artist. Unfortunately the details of my situation were less glossy. I was living inside a drafty bat-ridden barn with no precise idea of where I was and no money. My bed was an old army cot. "Had me a lot of great loving on that bed," my sculptor had told me. I supposed I was to imagine him bringing my predecessors into this vast empire of batshit and cement, and rocking and rolling with them while empty plastic wine bottles danced on the floor. For me, alas, the cot was only a piece of loose canvas slung unconvincingly between two metal pipes, just high enough off the cement floor to allow easy passage for the rats I was sure must be sneaking around the barn at night.

My sculptor had gone on vacation and I was broke, lost and feeling sorry for myself. The barn was unused because his farm had been turned into a watercress plantation.

The original family—a huge group of sixteenth-century peasants dressed in smudged blue denim—still lived in the adjoining buildings. I shared a courtyard and the prehistoric outhouses I'd been given permission to use with them and their domestic animals.

I didn't yet speak French, couldn't keep clean, didn't know how to leave. My only escapes were the local tavern, where in addition to being seen as Canadian I was considered a linguistic moron, and another farmhouse a couple of miles away where a fellow "apprentice" was doing odd jobs for a cartoonist. Why didn't I borrow some money from my friend and leave? First, because he had none. Second, because without money I had nowhere to go. Finally, because I was—as I would be so many times later in life—transfixed and paralyzed by the impossibility of my situation. I couldn't think clearly, couldn't act.

Meanwhile I could eat because I was allowed to put my groceries on the sculptor's account at the local store, I could do a little plastering while waiting to be released, I could even think about how, if I ever got out, this adventure could be related in a more favourable light.

There was one other reason I needed to stay where I was. I needed to know what was going to happen between me and my pads of blank paper. I wasn't a wild-haired student radical any more. I wasn't Hemingway in baggy cords. I wasn't even Henry Miller or T.S. Eliot or Anaïs Nin. I wasn't anyone at all—just a blank, a mute exile, a test case on whether the fantasy I'd had about writing a novel was a rhetorical gimmick useful for talking to blonde English majors, or whether there was a novel inside me to be written. In the end, I wrote because I was lonely and I needed to hear voices and I was the only possible source. I wrote because writing was the only way I knew to fill the weeks between the indeterminate now and the unknown day when my sculptor would return with, I fervently hoped, a letter from home containing money. I wrote because, having started to tell myself a story to fill the emptiness, I wanted to find out what would happen next.

Every night I would make myself a tomato omelet and wash it down with poisonous cheap red wine. By dark the universe would have shrunk to a small place that contained only me, the army cot I was sitting on, the sputtering candles lighting the pages to which I applied myself. Time was the march of ink across the page. So long as it continued so did I.

Eventually my sculptor came back, bearing food, apologies and an armload of mail, which included money from my parents and the offer of a scholarship to do my master's degree in political science at the University of Toronto. By this time the designated barn wall had been transformed, albeit clumsily, from a pitted stone reminder of the Middle Ages to a large white plaster blank. And my notebooks had gathered a huge poem about my favourite subject, a lovestruck young man walking in the rain to the tune of his unrequited love, and several chapters of a novel about, coincidentally, a young musician whose rain-inspired melodies echoed, etc.

By the end of August I was in London spending the nights in pubs with university friends. I caught a taste of Carnaby Street after all: my time in rural France became a rollicking series of misadventures it took at least three drinks to relate.

In the meantime I was showing bits of my "novel" around. A family friend of a classmate, who claimed that his mistress worked for the venerable publishing house Faber & Faber, read it enthusiastically and loaned it to a wealthy friend. He and the friend then made me an extraordinarily generous offer: they would subsidize me while I finished the novel and got it published. For a few days I believed I would stay on in London. Why I didn't I don't know. Perhaps the time in the sculptor's barn had exhausted my desire to be with my muse. Or maybe being dependent on the generosity of others was more than my suspicious soul could bear. By September I was back at the university, financially self-sufficient for the first time in my life, but with a lingering fear that by not staying on in London I had betrayed the only chance I would ever have to get off the academic treadmill and do something I truly cared about.

The

Sixties

----

how the escape broadens and
a new terrain and possible
identities are invented

I first began to pay attention to George Grant the day Jim Laxer walked into a political meeting holding aloft, like a newly discovered Bible, his copy of Grant's treatise on Canada's failure to exist, *Lament for a Nation*. Laxer (now a well-known writer and political commentator) would later become one of the leaders of the Waffle, a radical NDP splinter group whose eventual demise foretold the ultimate failure of the NDP itself. But in 1965 he was a walking visual contradiction: an eloquent and committed left-wing student of history and political science with what I considered to be the bizarre habit of always dressing in a blue blazer and flannels.

In those days political meetings of the left, whatever their formal agenda, mostly consisted of people sitting around in a room interrupting each other. It was the perfect format for shallow anarchistic types (such as myself) for whom the height of political wisdom was to throw digressive one-liners into the discussion that made everyone forget whatever it was they were attempting to discuss.

"This book!" Laxer exclaimed. "Everyone must read this book!"

He waved it about as though introducing the Messiah. When no one reacted I took it from him and began leafing through it.

At the time I knew very little about Grant, except that he was a philosophy professor, and that he had left York University for McMaster because he objected to being forced to use as a text the book written by Marcus Long (the very teacher who had drunkenly signed the form allowing me to switch from science to arts). I also knew that he had been speaking out publicly against the Americans' conduct of the war in Vietnam. Flipping through the pages of *Lament for a Nation*, my initial reaction was to dismiss him. The text seemed to be a clarion call for a forgotten brand of nineteenth-century conservatism, a political doctrine I associated with stuffy old British gentry spouting off while drinking port after a hard day hunting foxes or robbing widows and orphans.

A few months later, I was meeting Grant almost every week and staying up all night reading the texts he demanded I master: Nietzsche, Freud, Leo Strauss, Kant, Heidegger, Hobbes, Plato, Jacques Ellul. As both curious reader and a student of political philosophy I had run into some of their books before. To me they were an often indecipherable hodge-podge with no visible points of reference, but to Grant they were a slowly unfolding exposé of how Western civilization had destroyed its own roots and values.

The virtue of Canada, according to Grant, was that it had once stood apart from the United States' purely technological empire. Thanks to its British inheritance (though that too was corrupt, Grant was later to write) Canada had embodied at least a remnant of those Western values that had been destroyed in the United States by what he called the technocracy. Grant believed that the United States was fuelled by the will to pure technique. No matter what "values" it gave lip service to, its core philosophy was that the passionate pursuit of material well-being and power need be restrained and inhibited by nothing.

Hypnotized both by his prophetic manner and the incredible clarity with which he viewed the development of Western thought, Grant's students were eager to prove him wrong—to prove that Canada could stand outside America's empire-building wickedness and be an island of virtue in a sea of condos.

Grant, touched and amused, and of course wanting to believe, encouraged young political activists even while he remained sceptical. It should have been obvious to us, especially after the publication of *Technology and Empire*, that his eye was on the long view, and that rather than being a political activist he was a philosopher committed to describing, not overturning, his own society; but our eyes were on our own lives and prospects.

Did we want to live in a material wasteland? Of course not! Did we want to see ourselves as mere appendages of the technocratic flowering of mindless bureaucracies? No! We wanted to be in charge of our own destiny. We wanted to believe in the future—and we were arriving at our vision of this future just as the whole country was beginning to be stirred by similar visions. Eventually these would be exploited by Pierre Trudeau, laudably bilingual and ambiguous. Trudeau, who would fan the fire of Canadian self-consciousness and stand as a symbol of Canadian nationalism, was in fact the anti-nationalist leader of the continentalist Liberal party; neither the left nor Canadian cultural nationalists ever had any reason to regard him as an ally. Yet he *was* at least arguing about what Canada should be—as were those who wanted an independent country. Had I been able, at my most confident moments, to foresee that the entire ground of political debate was about to disappear from beneath my feet I might have better understood the bemused scepticism with which Grant listened to the ravings of his disciples.

My first encounter with Grant began as inauspiciously as had my first encounter with *Lament for a Nation*.

It took place in a large co-op house I was sharing with several others. (I would later discover that this very house, and indeed the very bedroom I occupied, had once been the residence from 1941 to 1946 of the writer Graeme Gibson. In 1965 he was pursuing his own student whirlwind and writing a novel called *Five Legs*.) The meeting was billed as an exploratory discussion between various New Left activists and George Grant. By then, I had read *Lament for a Nation*. Nonetheless, I showed up late. By the time I arrived the large living room was jammed with denim-clad cigarette-smoking students.

They were all talking at once, as usual. But though Grant couldn't be heard, he could certainly be seen. Physically massive—well over six feet and weighing in at over a hundred kilos—he was sitting in the middle of the sofa at the back of the room, head rotating to face the various speakers, listening with the utmost attention and care. In one of his large hands he held a cigarette; most of its ashes, along with the ashes of many predecessors, trailed down the vest and jacket of what must once have been a perfectly respectable navy three-piece suit.

My encounter with Grant was in many ways decisive for my life. I was twenty-two years old and drifting in almost every sense. Although I was a graduate student with scholarships, I suspected that my university "success" was due less to my so-called intellect than to the sudden expansion of graduate schools to provide enough professors to cope with the rising tide of baby boomers now invading the classrooms. Although I was delighted to have been chosen for something, I could not picture myself standing in front of a class posing as an expert in some field about which I knew virtually nothing. But other than writing, no career had presented itself. And in Canada at that time, writing was not a career in any sense.

At the same time, my political activities had begun to strike me as more comical than anything else. Although I completely agreed with the general intent of the student radicals with whom I was associated, I was unable to believe that North America was on the verge of a revolution. In fact, in 1965, it hadn't even occurred to me that significant social change might be on its way. Of course, along with tens of thousands of others of my generation, I was certain that the established order was about to collapse. My problem was that I was convinced that if it did collapse it would be replaced not by the kind of utopia I would prefer, but by something even more sinister and authoritarian. It's the kind of thought one has when one has been reading too many history books—a mistake many of my co-activists had avoided.

By the time of the meeting with Grant I felt as though I had one foot in and one foot out of "the movement." I wasn't about to leave, because I had nowhere else to go, but I wasn't sure that I still had a role to play.

Grant was obviously an advocate of social justice, but he was opposed to the materialist basis of Marxism. However, our common cause against the Vietnam War turned out to be enough to justify discussions of future projects, and the meeting ended—like so many meetings—with an agreement to meet again in order to discuss exactly what these projects might be.

As I'd arrived late, I was standing at the back, and was the one in a position to let Grant out the door. We introduced ourselves, and then, as we were standing chatting on the side porch of the house, Grant—with a shout of recognition and laughter—pointed to a window across the driveway. As excited as if he had discovered an amazing artefact, he explained that once (perhaps it had been with Graeme Gibson's parents) he had been standing on this exact same porch, looking at that exact same window, when the blind popped up and one of his professors was revealed doing calisthenics in his underwear.

This memory put Grant into such an excellent mood that he asked me if one could get a coffee and a sandwich anywhere nearby, since he wanted to refuel before driving back to Hamilton. I was hungry, as always at that age, and suggested we walk down to the corner and have a milkshake.

With his thick grey-blond hair, his blue eyes, his rosy cheeks, his disgracefully unkempt clothes, Grant was like an enormously overgrown and very mischievous choirboy who had somehow escaped school for the afternoon. As we walked down the street, it became clear that to him Toronto was *terra cognita*. By bloodlines, birth, upbringing, and political and family connections, Grant was part of what I saw as the British-Canadian ruling establishment, whose authoritarian nature and anti-Semitism had frequently rung extremely sour notes in my life.

So, to begin with, Grant was clearly the enemy. On the other hand, Grant was also clearly a friend. Supposedly a student of political philosophy, I had read enough to be able to "listen intelligently" to Grant's attack on liberalism and to add my own comments. Grant, an extraordinary conversationalist, didn't simply give a dry analysis of a book. He stepped into the ring with it, and like Muhammad Ali surrounded it with such a dizzying barrage of puns, feints, classical references, ad hominems, deadly blows to the vital organs and fancy toe-tapping attacks to vulnerable places it had not appeared to have, that in the end the poor thing simply collapsed, destroyed by the weight of its own history, by ridicule, and by its own complete blindness to the truly essential.

Grant, the conversationalist, created instant mayhem. And yet he always knew exactly what he thought. Like many charismatic people he was a master of rhetoric and polemic. Behind the apparent verbal confusion the train was always moving closer, and when it finally arrived at the station—triumphant, majestic, all the cars in the right order—Grant would lean back and smile, a magician pleased with his work.

I (the would-be writer) was instantly dazzled by these linguistic pyrotechnics. And by the time we arrived at the restaurant, the George Grant of the sparely written *Lament for a Nation* (a book I admired but considered to be about a kind of Canada whose loss didn't at the time seem entirely tragic to me) had been replaced by a man who inhabited a political and linguistic terrain I couldn't yet discern but knew I wanted to learn about.

> Western technical achievement has shaped a civilization different from any previous, and we North Americans are the most advanced in that achievement. This achievement is not simply something external to us. . . . It moulds us in what we are . . . not only in the heart of our animality . . . but in our actions and thoughts and imaginings. . . . Through that achievement we have become the heartland of the wealthiest and most powerful empire that has yet been. We can exert our influence over a greater extent of the globe and take a greater tribute of wealth than any previously.

Few readers will know the above lines. They are from the opening of "In Defence of North America," the first essay in Grant's *Technology and Empire*. Although *Lament for a Nation* was the best-known of his books, the most influential was *Technology and Empire*, almost entirely because of these first lines in which Grant posits that our actual *human being* has been taken over and transformed by the soulless modern world.

Grant saw North America as a Roman-style empire, complete with bloody wars, colonies from which it milked money, and a populace kept in a state of mind-numbed acquiescence. This perception dovetailed perfectly with the beliefs of sixties anti-war activists who were growing their hair long while awaiting the revolution, made jokes about the mind police and were devotedly opposed to the American war in Vietnam.

In the United States, the fact that Grant's thesis had neither class analysis nor racial conflict at its centre prevented him from becoming the major figure he was here; in Canada, however, such omissions, at least at that time, appeared less important.

Grant had articulated three related ideas that people had begun to think about but hadn't really grasped. First, that the United States wasn't simply enjoying a postwar boom, but had continued growing and developing as a military and industrial power to the point where it not only dominated the non-Communist nations of the world, but was also intimately involved in manipulating many or most aspects of all of these nations' lives.

Second, that although Canadians might prefer to keep their hands clean, they were clearly part of this empire and shared geography, resources, technology and financial benefits.

Third, that this American empire was not only a political holding, it was also a way of life—Western enlightenment packaged and communicated (the medium is the message) by Tinseltown itself. Thirty years later, we can see how prescient Grant was. Not that it matters, because the reality of our situation as powerless and passive onlookers of an enormous empire is that whatever we think is of absolutely no consequence—the vast majority of the population is much more interested in embracing the new reality, no matter how poisonous to their own real interests, than in a hopeless struggle against it.

A social conservative, a committed family man, a committed Christian, George Grant did not have as much in common with his admirers as they wanted to believe. They were fascinated by him because he took them seriously and could clearly articulate ideas they sensed but couldn't properly say.

He was fascinated by them because he saw them as possibly noble savages who might rebel against their masters, and he approved of such rebellions. He also believed that given the real balance of power their resistance was doomed from the beginning, but this didn't shake his conviction that their cause was a good one—Grant was looking at the larger picture, from the longer view.

My years at the Spadina Road apartment where I met George Grant were the peak of my self-declared immortality. On December 30, 1965, I turned twenty-three, which meant that two more immortal years remained.

Life was both disastrous and perfect. Personal relationships were a constantly evolving catastrophe. On the one hand I always felt that I was the victim; on the other, I was completely detached and indifferent. Such schizophrenia was easy for me at the time. So was everything. I had, after all, the great good fortune to be living in the centre of the universe, on Spadina Road.

Spadina was Toronto Central, the cosmic spine. On its southern stretch, you could breakfast at the Crest Grill, lunch at Switzer's, dine, drink beer and listen to jazz at Grossman's Tavern. You could shoot pool on Spadina, walk with girlfriends on Spadina, you could, like a photographer I knew, decide to spend six months taking a picture of the Spadina-College intersection every half hour. I myself had already lived at three Spadina addresses, eaten at a dozen Spadina restaurants, dressed in Spadina-bought clothes, even gone to my grandfather's funeral at a Spadina Avenue funeral chapel. Two years later I would be walking through the snow towards this very same house—looking fondly at my new car parked on the front lawn. Another car, speeding south, would slide off the road and crunch into my door on the driver's side. Had I been sitting in my own car on my own front lawn, listening to the news or having a sleep or a picnic, I could have been killed. Another day, from exactly the same spot on the corner of Lowther and Spadina, I would look down at a newspaper box and see LBJ WON'T SEEK RE-ELECTION in black letters across the front page of the *Toronto Daily Star*.

But when I turned twenty-three, I did not yet own a car. Lyndon Johnson was still everyone's father's hero. My own father had recently written to advise me to quit wasting my life as a misguided student activist: Lyndon Johnson, he predicted, would be remembered for his prescience in Vietnam. My father need not have worried: I was no longer wasting my life as a student activist. I was wasting it in numerous other ways, which he either didn't know about or was tactfully ignoring. I was wasting it as fast as I could, which was never fast enough, and that was how I liked it.

For some reason I remember waking up on the New Year's morning after my birthday. It was noon. Time to pull on my jeans, light a cigarette, contemplate the fact that I was twenty-three years and two days old, look at my Olivetti standing emptily on the desk and contemplate the fact that since I'd returned from my summer in Europe, fiction had deserted me—no doubt because by trading my barn for the comforts of paid graduate school, I had also turned my back on it.

I opened the window. A few gritty snowflakes blew onto my bare feet. Someone on the first floor was playing the piano and the notes fell around me like drops from the fountain of youth. Not that I needed them, since I was already immortal, but maybe the only time you find things like the fountain of youth is when you don't need them. I finished dressing and went out to stand on the sidewalk. I could see the piano player: in a red paisley smoking jacket he was hunched over his baby grand, pounding his way through a mountain of Rachmaninoff crescendos. The sky glowed a nasty January pearly grey. I loved it. A bus passed, spewing exhaust. I sucked it in happily. This was Toronto, 1966. The very first day—and by now the sixties, the fabulous and unpredictable sixties, had grabbed hold of my consciousness and ignited me with their crazy optimism.

I began walking toward Bloor Street. Toronto had stopped being Hogtown, but it hadn't yet promoted itself to world class. A comfortably well-off provincial city, self-consciously slathered in make-up and well provided with complacently chubby purses just begging to be sucked hollow by worthy causes, Toronto was incredibly more than it seemed: an infinity of delectable possibilities, an adolescent theme park throbbing with folk music, jazz, drugs, protest marches, idealists of all ages, delusions of grandeur, delusions of wealth, delusions of righteousness. Despite the fact that I was wasting my life, despite the fact that the very bed I rose from was emptier than it should have been because the woman with whom I'd recently been sharing it had decided to go waste her own life with someone else, despite the fact I had no idea whom to see, what to do or how to pay for something to eat, I couldn't have been happier.

Almost three months later, on a snowy March night, the sixties flipped a switch I hadn't known was there. It was three o'clock in the morning. I was with Oliver T. in the basement of his parents' house. I had met Oliver a few years before, when we were both members of the university ban-the-bomb club, officially known as the Combined Universities Campaign for Nuclear Disarmament, the one with the little peace pins that looked like an upside-down Y. Oliver had joined because, like his parents, he was a pacifist. I had joined because as a child I'd been kept home from school one day to watch a television program starring an atomic blast, and shortly after that I'd come across a book of photographs of Hiroshima survivors.

At three in the morning, Oliver said, "I have something special for tonight's agenda," and pulled out Bob Dylan's new homage to electricity. After setting it on the turntable he opened a drawer and withdrew three of those fat, funny-looking cigarettes we had been warned about in high-school health class. I'd often tried them before and found them mildly pleasant, hangover free, and conducive to sharpening the appetite and listening to music. In short, an excellent alternative to drinking and a worthwhile addition to late-night life, but nothing to make a fuss about.

But this time would be different.

At dawn we were in the ravine below the St. Clair Reservoir, and the pale gold and silver light off the snow had first filled my body, then dissolved my skin and scattered me across the city. In those days, in middle-of-the-night Toronto, the only person you needed to be afraid of running into was yourself. I sat down at the base of a tree, leaned my head back and looked up at the sky. Bob Dylan was wired into my brain. I closed my eyes and waited for enlightenment. It arrived: I realized I was sitting beside the biggest toilet tank in all of Ontario. If someone pulled the right chain, the entire city would be flushed into the lake.

An hour later I was driving down cosmic Spadina to return my borrowed car to its owner. Just north of Bloor Street I noticed I had lost control of my hands and feet. The yellow Toronto morning sky had turned blue, bricks glowed as though lit from the inside, and every passing rush-hour face was broadcasting its life story in my direction. Meanwhile, the car I had been driving seconds ago, the borrowed car that I was supposedly returning, was continuing, governed by the laws of inertia and chance, at about twenty miles an hour in the direction of its usual parking spot. Unfortunately, a police car was directly in front of me. Governed by its own laws, including a red light, it was stopped. By a miracle my car stopped behind it. The steely, inquiring gaze of the law did a carefully angled bank off its rear-view mirror and tried to pierce through the centres of my thick lenses. I felt like Peter

Rabbit caught in Mr. McGregor's garden. The light changed, and after a brief harrowing drive my borrowed car was back in place, and I was on foot. I was standing on Spadina just north of the circle, the yellow eye of the sun had risen above the university and the blue slushy morning was pouring in, louder than Niagara Falls. Immortality. When I got home I put a yellow sheet of paper in my Olivetti and for the first time in almost two years I began typing a short story.

The next week I was with George Grant, walking by the very spot where my borrowed car almost crashed. We were on our way from to Bloor Street's Riviera Restaurant, at that time justly famed for its "old-fashioned" milkshakes, sundaes and banana splits, which combined maximum volume with minimum price. Grant looked around the crowded intersection and asked what for him was the obvious question: "Why are the young reading Nietzsche instead of Plato?"

"Because," I replied, "it is more interesting to destroy than to build."

Grant sighed contentedly.

Had I known more about the power of the European youth movements in the nineteenth century, I would have understood that Grant was searching for a historical parallel, but at the time I saw his fascination with "the young" as the excitement of a committed teacher presented with the blank slate of minds unspoiled by exposure to wrong (or any!) ideas. Almost before we did, Grant had tagged us, the sixties generation, as more open than our elders, and more prepared to challenge the assumptions of progress and liberalism, which Grant saw as merely the preferred propagandistic cant of an American capitalist empire that had disconnected itself from human reality in order to serve the necessities of technology. Did any of us understand what Grant meant? Did we care? Flattered and spellbound, unaware that for him "openness" and ignorance weren't unrelated, students clustered about him.

Since returning from my summer in the French barn, I had completed my master's in political theory. My dissertation had not been on the kind of topic that was fashionable at the time—perhaps a study of statistical techniques of polling or vote sampling—but on the political thought of Albert Camus. This was an excellent subject to write on while wearing baggy corduroys and thinking deep thoughts, but it served my literary curiosity a lot better than my potential career as a political scientist. Nonetheless, perhaps in recognition of my Quixotic idiocy in sacrificing my own best interests to what actually interested me, I was offered a full slate of fellowships to stay on and continue with my doctorate.

These studies involved first taking those courses that would lead to my comprehensive exams. Unfortunately, I had somehow lost interest in the whole enterprise. By the spring of 1966, my drift from the academic life had widened to the point where my main attachment to the university was spending its money. Meanwhile, I had replaced my official studies with trying to understand George Grant, a Christian Platonist whose real beliefs should have been entirely disagreeable to me. Between our meetings, aside from wandering the city, listening to Bob Dylan, smoking funny cigarettes and living various mutually contradictory lives, I obsessively read all the books Grant mentioned and began to write tract-like elaborations of the clumsy replies I gave to his questions.

As spring turned to summer I spent hours every day sitting at my trusty portable olive-coloured Olivetti, pounding away with two fingers and covering sheet after sheet of yellow paper with single-spaced rants. Why? Because it was fun. Because I had nothing else to do. Because sex, music and politics were my Bermuda Triangle in Toronto, 1966.

By August, the triangle had taken its toll. Once again my personal life collapsed, and I'd moved out of the centre of the universe to a basement apartment on Walmer Road. My landlady was a reflexologist who claimed that foot-rubbing, along with frequent use of her sauna, could cure any disease. Mine was mononucleosis. It had come on me over a series of weeks, leaving me feverish and hallucinating strange people who came after me wielding knives and large shears with shiny cutting edges. I lost twenty pounds and I actually began to question whether wasting my life was, after all, such a desirable idea.

One August day, walking down Yorkville, now known as "the village" and thronging with the new crowd who wore peace buttons and paid real money to buy various kinds of equipment for smoking dope, I felt so dizzy and confused that I had to stop to lean against a post. A woman came up to me, offering a paper cup of lemonade. Then she told me I looked "thin and haunted" and that "a cosmic struggle" was taking place in my soul. It turned out she was into Buddhistic group therapy and costume jewellery. After an intense discussion about birth dates, she gave me a beautiful brass Capricorn pendant complete with leather thong.

A week later, wearing sandals and my most faded jeans, I went to visit her. She made us herbal tea in her kitchen. I played the guitar. She sat in a rocking chair and suggested we go on a Buddhist retreat at a hermitage north of Toronto. I imagined myself trudging through the mountains of Tibet, a Capricorn goat ascending the thin air toward the sun. Then she wanted to talk about the revolution. She had been to hear Stokely Carmichael talk about Black Power. Me, too. He was infinitely brave, enraged, articulate. Powerful: full of power. Black activists and civil-rights workers needed to be full of power to confront the forces that would crush them. But much as I admired and applauded the way the civil rights movement had empowered itself, I was certain that power is dangerous, that power invades the core of your beliefs, that power wants you to become the mirror of your enemy. Within what had first been the peace movement, then the anti-war and civil rights movement, nonviolence had gone from belief to strategy to tactic.

"The revolution is coming," I said to my new friend. And then, echoing Trotsky, "We live in the time of permanent revolution." She poured me another cup of herbal tea. What I really believed was that the revolution, whatever that was, was over. Although I wasn't going to say it to her, she could have seen that obvious truth the afternoon we met on Yorkville Avenue: the revolution, or whatever it had been, had changed right in front of our eyes from something people did together, because they wanted to, into something people were selling and buying. One day the continent might explode in rage or collapse, but not yet, not soon.

Walking home I surfed the waves of my fellow "young." We all had our faded jeans, our pendants, our sandals and untamed hair. But the revolution had turned into the diesel fumes that floated like mist through the streets, the dust that caked our bare feet and ankles. Everyone was stoned or wanted to be or was pretending to be or was growing groovy beards to look like Jesus or wearing tie-dyed skirts and Mary Magdalene hair and looking at each other through dewy eyes. By the time the summer of 1966 drew to a close, you couldn't go out the door without meeting thousands of "the young" winking at each other out of their bottomless glowing wells of Beatles-inspired enlightenment and the peace that passeth understanding. Feeling thin and haunted, I went back to see my rocking-chair friend. She said, "You pretend to be a cynic. Really what you want is to believe in love. But you can't."

I tried to explain that Ottawa Jews probably can't turn themselves into Toronto hippies. The term "Ottawa Jew" made her light a stick of incense and take out what she promised was some very special imported herbal tea. We sat on the porch and listened to sitar music while the light fell out of the sky. When it was dark we went and lay down on her bed. Thanks to the special tea, her room had become a spaceship, her bed an enclosed platform in a rocket waiting to blast off to an undiscovered planet. We went into a black tunnel. At first it was the Tunnel of Endless Pleasure. Then it was simply a tunnel, simply pleasure, simply endless, simply black. I began to think that this was why "the young" read Nietzsche, that somewhere in this tightly wound spiral of pleasure, pain, infinite exhaustion and energy was where God must have died. Or dissolved in confusion.

Afterward she put on her sunglasses and made ordinary tea. "Naked woman with sunglasses," I said. She laughed. We drove through the city, the air moving through the leaves in a way it never would again. For the first time I had been with someone to whom some unspeakable violence had been done. What it was, I didn't know. Nor had she spoken of it. But it had left her a refugee, haunting the ruins of her own bombed-out city. She, I realized, was on the firm ground of suffering and pain accepted and overcome—ground that I could never know. I felt like a tourist.

"I feel like a tourist," she said. Like that.

She left me at my basement apartment. I went in and looked at my olive-coloured Olivetti, the keys lined up in rows, waiting. After the March epiphany I was writing fiction again, and yellow sheets filled with attempts at short stories had been making their way from my typewriter to my wastebasket. But this particular story wasn't one I was yet ready to write. Or even begin to think about.

In the fall of 1966 I went to a meeting of the education committee of what would one day be a high-rise student residence called Rochdale College. Rochdale was still a year away from the beginning of construction, but its mortgage as an "educational institution" had been approved, and for that purpose politicized graduate students were useful on its lists of committees. Rochdale began life as an offshoot of Campus Co-op and various of its representatives were at the meeting. Also U of T professor and future Waffle leader Mel Watkins, representing what might be termed the Almost Responsible Left; students from various student-elected councils, representing the Voice of the People; and finally myself, supposed radical political activist, representing the Unpredictable Element. We didn't yet know it, but the Unpredictable Element would eventually throw Rochdale totally off course. But it wouldn't be me or people like me. It would be—and who could have predicted it?—those peace-symbol-decorated teenagers from all over the province who were starting to run away from home and flood Yorkville in search of new lives fuelled by friendship, love and creativity. Who can blame them? In my own way I was doing the same thing, but because I was older the homes I ran away from were my own.

While Rochdale was being constructed, more than five hundred of these runaways would move into the building. Known as crashers, they slept in unoccupied rooms and in the halls. Many of them would live there until Rochdale, whose architects had had the prescience to make the halls wide enough for two lanes of wheelchairs, became a home for senior citizens. The runaway from his own house who was me would also end up at Rochdale, and one of my jobs would be to take a survey of the crashers who had crashed the party; the survey would discover that sixty-three per cent of them intended to be professional dancers.

At the education committee meeting, everyone was smoking cigarettes. Real ones. By this stage of the sixties, I had learned that any meeting dominated by people whose cigarette of choice could be bought in a store was a meeting worth leaving.

Outside, the leaves were thick on the sidewalks and lawns. I was only a few steps from where Rochdale would some day rise, and eventually be mythologized as a high-rise haven for drug dealers who rode their motorcycles into the elevators, a castle of evil protected by a moat of dogshit deposited by their dope-and-fire-breathing kill-trained Nazi studded-collar Dobermans and German shepherds. But I had no visions of this, no visions at all. I walked along Bloor Street to a Coles bookstore that glowed with the fluorescent yellow ambience of Coles Notes. I scanned the notes for *The Return of the Native*, which I had studied in high school. *Had an observer witnessed a certain undistinguished gentleman flipping through the notes of a book he was clearly unable to remember* . . . I said to myself. Perhaps at the next meeting of the education committee, I could raise the possibility of Rochdale financing itself by Rochdale Notes for the Uninitiated. *The Revolution: As in "Come the revolution," a phrase followed by the name of the person to be shot.* I left the store and went upstairs to the apartment above, where two friends lived. It was ten in the evening, their normal visiting hours. They had all their LPs spread out on the floor, and explained to me they had decided to arrange them in alphabetical order. We ended up sitting at the window with the curtains open and the lights out, watching the Bloor Street traffic as though it were a movie, remembering favourite scenes from *Dr. Strangelove*, and discussing who really killed JFK.

At one in the morning I was on the street again. As usual, these nights. I couldn't go home before walking down Spadina, that old cosmic spine no longer mine, and looking up at the window of a girl I wished was my girl-friend. Her sash was partly raised, curtains waved gently in the breeze, her light was off. Twice I'd been inside that room, looking out. Small and perfect encounters after which she had said goodbye in a tone that implied not a day or a week, but eternity. Now I could imagine her inside her room, wearing her pink bunny-covered nightie and having a long, healthy sleep. I wished she would wake up, discover me on the street, invite me into her room, into her life. She had a life. In her life everything made sense. That was something I firmly believed in those years: that all those Toronto windows, lighted or dark, contained lives filled with some kind of central reality and order. Except mine. I wasn't inside a lighted room, sleeping or typing on my Olivetti or studying for my comprehensives. Instead I was exiled from myself, doomed to roam the streets looking enviously at other people's windows until I was too exhausted to walk. Then finally I'd retreat to my basement apartment, try reading a dozen different books, writing a letter to eternity or a tract or three. Sometimes there might be three-in-the-morning visits from or to the few others I knew who lived this same absurd schedule. We'd end up washed into the morning like so much drift-wood, falling asleep to the music of rush-hour traffic.

On my twenty-fourth birthday I received two phone calls. One was from my rocking-chair friend. She had abandoned costume jewellery for the tarot, and on my birthday she read my soul. "You are a born mystic," she told me. "Your spirit seeks its Other." The second call was from the girl with the window. Eternity had shrunk, the small perfect visits had multiplied, but then she had said goodbye a final time and moved out west. She was calling from Vancouver, just wanting me to know that she hadn't forgotten me. "But you could forgive me," I suggested. She laughed, and I'll always remember the sound of her voice, two thousand miles of pure surprise that for an instant tore away all the silly games we'd played with each other and let me believe that whatever we'd done, it was only to amuse and console each other. This may have been the most optimistic moment of my life. For months afterward I bored everyone I knew saying I was about to toss all my possessions in my car, drive to where she was living and throw myself at her feet.

A few weeks after my birthday, when immortality had only a year to go, something happened that would turn out to be absolutely unique in my life: I was offered a full-time, permanent job. Even though I couldn't know this was the only job I'd ever be offered (I still read the careers section in the newspaper every morning) I was suitably shocked.

I was at George Grant's house in Dundas, Ontario, a large and comfortable nineteenth-century relic located on a couple of overgrown acres. Despite its size, the place was easily filled by Grant, his wife, and their six children. As usual we were sitting in his living room and having "tea," which in addition to the tea itself included a never-ending series of plates of sandwiches, which all three of us—me, Grant and his wife, Sheila—would hungrily attack until they evolved into plates of pastries and sweets, which were equally welcome.

"I and the university would truly be honoured if you would accept this position," George Grant said, having described the opening in the McMaster department of religion that he proposed I could fill. "There's only one problem," he added.

I thought he was going to tell me I had to finish my doctoral dissertation. This was an enterprise I had not even started since I had not been allowed to choose a topic irrelevant to the interests of the department (as I had for my master's) and none of the suitable topics were of any interest to me. It wasn't that I feared a statistically oriented topic—even after I'd switched into arts I had continued to take statistics courses. The problem was that over the years I had become so selfish and spoiled in my intellectual interests that I only wanted to spend my time pursuing whatever currently fascinated me. I have to admit this vice has haunted me all my life. I've never been able to write a book I didn't want to, even one I thought might make a lot of money. Even writing a six-hundred-word review of a book I don't like is an arduous task. So that afternoon, faced with what I feared would be an impossible demand, I said nothing. In fact, I was incapable of speaking.

But, as it turned out, the problem was that McMaster had once been a Baptist college.

"I don't mind," I said. "I'm very tolerant."

"Ah yes," Grant said. "But, you know, many of the people working at McMaster University are left over from those days."

"Well, I probably won't have much to do with them," I said.

"One of them is the dean. You'll have to be screened by him before the department can offer you the position officially."

"I'll wear a tie."

By this time Grant was starting to look anxious, and he and Sheila were exchanging glances. I realized that I had always dressed extremely informally for our meetings, but neither Grant nor Sheila had ever seemed the type to stand on ceremony, and Grant himself was constantly joking about whether this or that occasion would require him to put in his teeth. In any case, I felt no anxiety over the clothing issue. I actually owned quite a nice sports jacket and pair of flannels. Since I only wore them once every year or two, they were in perfect condition. And my friend above the bookstore had a great collection of school and regimental ties.

"It's about your being Jewish," Grant said. "He doesn't like Jews."

"My name gives me away," I conceded. "But isn't it illegal to refuse to hire Jews? Anyway, you already have at least one Jew in your department."

"He'll hire you," Grant said. "But it would be a lot easier if you didn't talk about it."

"About being Jewish."

"Yes."

I looked down into my teacup and imagined myself in the dean's office, dressed up in my spiffy clothes and borrowed tie. *Just a few weeks since Hanukkah*, I might remark, *did you get anything good?* Or: *I know this is supposed to be a job interview, but do you mind me asking if Baptists really believe all Jews go to Hell?* "It's okay," I said, "I think I'll be able to bite my tongue."

"Then it's settled," Grant said with a broad grin.

In the end I also agreed that I would attempt to complete my thesis, a task made easier by the fact that Grant consented to be one of my advisers. On that basis, he also gave his blessing to my plan to live in Toronto for the time being so that I could have easy access to the U of T library for research purposes.

When I'd passed the interview and the contract had been delivered and signed, I made two further decisions. One was to buy a red Volkswagen. I'd never owned a car but would need one now to drive back and forth from Hamilton. The second was to move back onto the cosmic spine: the personnel at my old co-op had rotated, a friend who was also a graduate student at McMaster had taken over half of it with his girlfriend, and my old room had come free.

By the time the summer came I was back in the centre of the universe, I had a monthly paycheque and a car, and I was spending a certain amount of time every day in front of my green Olivetti writing not my thesis, alas, but more short stories. I still had not been able to actually *finish* a story since getting back from my French barn, but with each attempt I was getting closer to an ending—or at least further from the beginning.

In September I began my career as a professor of religion at McMaster University. I didn't actually know anything about religion, aside from what I'd learned in Hebrew school where, unfortunately, I never paid attention. But

Grant had already explained to me that my formal ignorance of the apparent subject was no problem. My actual teaching duties would be to give two courses: one in "the sociology of religion," which would be about systems of belief—something I could make up, in other words—and another that could be a lightly disguised graduate course in political philosophy. Of course, he explained, I was welcome to learn whatever I liked about actual religions. The department was filled with experts who would be glad to advise and discuss.

Fortunately, it was the sixties. When I announced to my students that all belief systems were based on power structures, and that I would demonstrate this by giving them the power—by making them take turns delivering the lectures—they found this entirely appropriate. It was even better when I told them that the last question on their final exam would be: What is your grade on this exam and why?

After a couple of months it became obvious that the main reason Grant had hired me was to provide himself with a conversational foil and amusement. At first I was insulted—hadn't he taken my teaching career seriously? Then I realized I myself had a contract and was free to take it as seriously as I wanted to. Some professors in the department were world experts in their fields. Others preferred making common cause with their students. It was up to me to make my own choices. All I had to do was keep up a minimum level of appearance and competence. On the other hand, continuing to meet and talk with Grant was no burden. On the contrary. By now I had begun to understand both the sweep and the details of his iconoclastic opposition to what he termed liberalism. His great project had been to retrace the intellectual history of the past several hundred years, understand the development of certain kinds of thought, and question the validity of what he took to be its very basis, the pure rationalism and accompanying belief in progress and technology that relegated "the good" to the status of a mere "value"—no more essential than a style of clothing or shade of lipstick.

Of course, thousands of other thinkers had also tried to understand the "modern," but there were two things about Grant that were very singular, at least to me. One was that like a very few other thinkers, such as Jacques Ellul and Leo Strauss, he had gotten *outside* the modern through his belief that there was a higher order of knowable truth, whether in fundamentalist Christianity or some version of semi-mystical Platonism. Like all great generals, Grant had rearranged the terrain in a way that was meaningless to his opponent but gave himself the highest and most impenetrable ground from which to launch his attacks.

The second: for whatever reason, Grant had chosen me as a person on whom to try out his various new formulations. "You'll disappoint him in the end," Sheila Grant once said to me, not without bitterness. And I knew immediately that she was correct. Unconventional though McMaster's department of religion was, Grant was nonetheless a kind of cult leader who demanded perfect faith and perfect fidelity. As such, he offered me the one path to salvation that in the end I could never take. That was why it was of interest to him to make the offer. I didn't have the background to counter his ideas with citations from philosophers or historical evidence, though of course I tried, and in trying I ended up getting an education. What I had that kept our conversations interesting for him was a quick tongue ready to defend a generational and cultural gap that could never be crossed. The truths Grant believed to be absolute were ideas I could not possibly assent to, because—and this would take me a very long time to figure out—to do so would be to betray the most irreducible essence of myself.

December 30, 1967, was my twenty-fifth birthday. Old age had now officially begun. Immortality was over. Time had carried me over the unthinkable divide. Otherwise, life wasn't so bad: I was still living on the cosmic spine, I had a red car, a job and a new girlfriend, Susie Bricker, with whom I was painfully and passionately involved. I was even starting to save some of the yellow pieces of paper that came out of my green Olivetti.

To celebrate my birthday and the end of youth, I'd decided to take an extended Christmas break from teaching in order to do "intensive sociological research." Accordingly, Susie and I equipped my car with studded tires—still legal at the time—loaded it with winter clothes and drove north from Toronto, over the top of Lake Superior and across the Prairies to a ten-acre field a few miles outside the Rocky Mountain town of Golden, B.C.

In the midst of that ten-acre field stood a one-room cabin. Its front vestibule had been converted into a privy, and part of one of the side walls had been punched out and extended into a bed-sized guest room made out of mill ends, through which snow slowly drifted during the long and icy nights.

The cabin belonged to friends who had, the year before, made their exodus from Toronto. They had laid out the details of this spectacular journey in George Grant's living room on the same day we had debated whether Bob Dylan or Mozart was a greater genius (Grant opted for Mozart). To Grant the idea that someone would simply walk away from job, family and unpaid credit cards was horrifying, romantic, appalling, but above all a magnificent affirmation of life he couldn't help admiring—whether or not he approved. His enthusiasm about action as opposed to verbiage, like his ideas about the political potential of "the young," had its roots in his reading of German romanticism, and was tied both to his rejection of rationalism and his fascination with Nietzsche. If I had better understood at the time that his philosophical position was based on thinkers who ultimately fuelled German nationalism, it would have made me extremely uncomfortable, but none of these ideas crossed my mind. I was happy to sit and listen as the renegade migrant-to-be disclosed that he was not only going off into the sunset, but also planning to tame wild mustangs and ride them through the Rocky Mountains. George was absolutely astounded, as I was. This was nature! This was life! This was Direct Contact with Reality! The one thing he admired about us nihilists was that our empty little centres tended to fill up with mystical experiences and wild enthusiasms. The more unreasonable our gestures the more Grant approved, both as an amused spectator and as a social analyst hoping there might be disruptive political possibilities in it.

"You're really going to do it!" Grant cackled. "Sheila, they're really going to do it!" More trays of sandwiches appeared, and on this historic day their crusts were trimmed. Putting down our tobacco pouches and cigarette papers (at the time it was politically necessary to roll one's own cigarettes, thus depriving multinational conglomerates of part of their profits) we devoured them, tray after tray.

When I reported on my friend's progress a few months later, Grant exclaimed, "Go visit him! You *must* visit him. Don't worry about your students. Go!"

When we arrived that frozen January, I realized Grant was right to regard this man with awe. Once a chain-smoking tweed-jacketed pale-faced febrile journalist, the migrant had evolved into a chain-smoking lumberjack-jacketed bare-handed gun-toting horse-riding master of the wilderness.

While I shivered and shook in my icy sleeping bag, the man of action leapt half-naked out of bed, grabbed an axe and went outside to split wood so his city guests would be warm enough to sleep in. (I later noticed that he had a goose-down sleeping bag, and that it was carefully positioned near the stove. But still . . .) When boredom struck in the afternoon, he and his newly and equally rusticated mate cantered across snow-covered fields on the horses they had reduced from wild beasts to domestic pets. And when my shiny new red Volkswagen froze solid at forty below, he cleverly made it start by jacking it up and building a fire beneath it to thaw out the engine.

"This is life!" I enthusiastically repeated to Grant on my return.

"Amazing!" Grant exclaimed. "He actually *rode* his horse across the mountains?"

"A wild horse. He broke it himself, at his friend's ranch."

"He rode a *wild* horse across the mountains!" Grant shouted gleefully. It was one of those days when shaving and teeth had been deemed unnecessary, and it wasn't hard to imagine Grant himself, enormously brawny and rumpled, leaning over some geezer campfire and recounting such exploits.

Speaking of life, or *life*, the trip west had confirmed my decision to start living my own. Teaching at McMaster was an amusing charade, but it couldn't go on. It was unfair to the students, who deserved better, and for myself it was just delaying the inevitable.

The sheets of yellow paper had piled up sufficiently that I was ready to believe that if I took a year, which could be financed by my savings from teaching, I would be able to finish writing a novel. What I would actually do with this novel if I wrote it was not a problem. Somewhere I still had the address of the man whose mistress read for Faber & Faber. I was still at an age and stage when I believed that stacks of paper necessarily transformed themselves into universally available hardcovers and mass-market paperbacks.

All I had to do was find the editorial mentor who could elevate my leaden scribblings into the gold of literature.

In the meantime, I needed to get rid of my job in order to have the purity of soul required to produce these leaden pages.

While I explained to Grant that my conscience impelled me to resign my position in order to be a writer, he listened with his usual careful, reserved attention, then asked me what it was exactly that I was going to write.

"A novel," I replied. "I've always wanted to write a novel."

"Aah," Grant sighed. "I love novels, I think they are the most noble form. Don't you agree, Sheila? Are not novels the highest form?"

Sheila considered this carefully. "There's opera," she finally said.

"And discourse," Grant added, "Platonic discourse. But it has the beauty of revelation, not the beauty of form."

"Henry James might have both," Sheila proposed. This was playing directly to Grant's own prejudices as he often stated how much he admired the work of Henry James.

"Yes, *The Golden Bowl*. Have you read *The Golden Bowl*? If you're going to write novels, you must read *The Golden Bowl*."

And that was it. No reproaches, no questions about how I would support myself, no reminders that I had signed a contract with the university. Only his insistence that I must read *The Golden Bowl*, which he would lend to me. He also offered to write a letter saying I was taking a year's leave of absence to do research (so that if I changed my mind I would still have a job waiting for me). And then Grant made a second offer, another amazing instance of his amazing generosity: he proposed that for the summer and into the fall, for as long as we could stand the cold, Susie and I could use the family cabin in Terrence Bay, Nova Scotia, as a place to live and write.

I drove away feeling as though I had just participated in an unexpected rewrite of *Julius Caesar*. I'd started the day certain that I was about to betray Grant and all the time and friendship he had given me, but he had reversed the situation and instead of falling mortally wounded to the floor, had given yet more. What it cost him to do so, I can never know. What it provided for me was the immeasurable gift of a platform of confidence and possibility.

Within a few months three more unexpected events had launched me on my career as a writer. Though of course I still hadn't written anything.

The first was that the education committee proposed that I play a continuing role at Rochdale College after it opened that coming fall, by moving in and giving seminars. When I explained that I had resigned from teaching in order to write my nonexistent novel, the proposal was adjusted: I would move in as "writer-in-residence."

The second was that a political article, actually a strange mixture of rant and fiction that I'd written for the Student Union for Peace Action (SUPA), which had been republished in what was then called *This Magazine Is About Schools*, was reprinted in an anthology from a brand new press called House of Anansi. I met, very briefly, the press's co-founder, Dennis Lee, at a political gathering. A few days later I ran into him on the street—*the* street, the cosmic spine where I still lived and where Anansi had had the instinctive good sense to locate itself.

Dennis was full of the news that Anansi had decided to start publishing fiction. In fact, he went on to say, they were searching for exciting new novels. I wouldn't, by chance, be writing one? Not only was I writing one, it was virtually complete, I assured him. (I had already assigned him the role of the mentor who could turn lead into gold.)

The third and decisive shoe was dropped, so to speak, when I tore the ligaments of my ankle playing basketball in the Clinton Street school yard. I spent the next two weeks in a cast in my room on Spadina (the very room once inhabited by Graeme Gibson, whose novel would be one of the first publications of the fledgling Anansi), in front of my green Olivetti, starting my novel.

Grant's "family cabin" turned out to be an extremely modest pre-fab cottage built on a small hill overlooking the south shore of Terrence Bay. It was one of the last of a final scattering of dwellings on the outskirts of the village, which ended, a couple of hundred yards away, at the lighthouse.

The cabin had a couple of bedrooms, a kitchen complete with traditional wood stove, and a large living room. The puzzle was where the large Grant family slept when they were in residence, and on what furniture, since the cabin had only a couple of beds, the stove, a dining-room table with a few chairs, a dilapidated couch. It turned out that one spring when the Grants weren't there, a grass fire had swept the area near the cabin and the people from the village had rushed to protect it. When it became evident that the fire was unstoppable and that the cabin was going

to be burned, they decided to at least save the furniture
and contents by carrying them to a safe distance. At that
point a wind came up and the fire changed direction, mer-
cifully saving the cabin but . . .

In any case, the furniture that remained was more than
enough for two young escapees from Toronto who had
never before lived by the sea. We bought drinking water
and kindling from the fishing family next door, we aug-
mented our wood supply by driving around and searching
for fallen pine boughs, which we hid in the car and smug-
gled up to the cabin in the dark lest we offend the neighbours, we ate fish we bought down at the docks, and of
course I continued work on my novel—by now turning
into a substantial manuscript, at least in volume, because
I had promised myself that part of the deal of deciding to
be a writer would be that, unlike so many other writers
I'd met, I would actually write. A minimum of a page and
a half a day, I'd decided, having read in a magazine that
Graham Greene, whose books I admired, made himself
write five hundred words a day. A page and a half doesn't
sound like much. But it was compulsory to write that minimum *absolutely every day*. Amazingly, given that I'd never
shown any signs of wanting or being able to make myself
do anything, I wrote that minimum at least 360 days a
year for over ten years. I also wasn't allowed to throw out
what I'd written. I didn't have to publish it, but I had to at
least keep it around and face it the next day.

As I got into the rhythm of writing, the spirit of self-
improvement came over me and I began to think perhaps

I should do something about my pitiful city boy's physical condition.

This came upon me one sunny day while we were driving down a rural road near the sea. The windows of my red McMaster-bought Volkswagen were open, scrub pine and telephone poles were piercing upwards into the liquid blue of the early evening sky. I was wearing steel-rimmed glasses and had long sideburns. Susie was wearing a batiked shirt and had hair below her shoulders. My belly was full of fish and chips and my eyes were on the telephone poles.

"You know," I said, "I used to be on the track team in high school."

"That's nice," Susie said.

"I've been thinking," I said, "that I ought to get into shape again."

"That's nice," she said.

"I suppose you don't believe me."

"Of course I believe you."

"I bet I could run a mile right now."

"Go ahead," she said.

I began counting telephone poles while watching the odometer. After twenty-eight I stopped the car and turned around. "All right," I said. "Drive back twenty-eight telephone poles and wait for me there."

I got out of the car and began to run, as slowly as possible. After three telephone poles I was breathing hard. Then I remembered that in high school I had only been the track team manager, but once I had actually come a close second in a race at a Hebrew school picnic. By the tenth telephone pole I was walking. When I came over a rise and in sight of the car I recommenced running. As I climbed in Susie put down her book and looked at her watch.

"How long did it take me?"

"Twenty-three minutes," she said.

Right then I vowed that before the summer was over I would run a mile without stopping. As the weeks went on I could feel my body, I thought, slowly gathering itself, refining itself, preparing to become a machine of awesome power and efficiency. I had absolutely no doubt that the magic moment would arrive and that I, a condensed and perfected version of myself, would be prancing through it, breathing easily, gliding like electricity from one pole to the next.

Until recently I could still run a mile. But the dream of perfect physical conditioning is—like being on the track team—a myth that belongs in the past rather than a goal to be arrived at in the future. All of these developments, I suppose, could have been foreseen. The one that couldn't, the one I can't get used to, is that the vision George Grant inspired in my generation has also rotated from future to past.

That I can even write such words amazes me. My first instinct is to qualify, moderate, revise, press a couple of buttons and have my word processor send that unwanted thought into electronic oblivion. How perfectly ironic Grant would find the notion of someone trying to clarify his thoughts about technology while staring into a monitor. Right beside me I even have his essay deriding the idea that computers are a "value-free" tool.

Not that I ever took what Grant said at face value: he himself encouraged the idea that every text presents itself as an amiable mask behind which more revolutionary sub-texts and codes are hidden. In our dozens of meetings we did nothing but debate such questions. During these dis-cussions Grant always listened, really *listened*, with such attentive expectation that I couldn't help hearing, really *hearing*, what I was saying. Which, I quickly realized, was mostly nonsense, rendered even more nonsensical by his enormous presence.

Among the many things I hadn't yet understood was that despite his fascination with subtexts, Grant also meant everything he wrote *exactly* as he wrote it. The hope that he inspired was the very hope he himself had given up as dated and illusory. That hope, on the surface, was that Canada could exist as a sovereign nation, and not as one whose prin-cipal goal was to integrate itself into the North American and world economies no matter the human consequences. (Can we imagine a Canadian government renouncing the idea of such an integration today?) The basis of that hope— the hope Grant was mourning as lost in *Lament for a Nation*—was that there had existed in Britain, and perhaps even in the United States, a philosophical conservatism ca-pable of balancing the drive and greed of pure capitalism. Now, thirty-five years later, after the long reign of Thatch-erism and Reaganism and the triumph of right-wing con-servatism, the idea that so-called market forces should be moderated by compassion and generosity, or that the pub-lic good and the needs of human community must counter-balance the arithmetic of greed, would be considered laughable by most of our political and corporate leaders.

Finally, as a subtext of the subtext—one that exists in all of Grant's work—there is an argument about the nature of human existence and history. George Grant believed that the Platonic account of human existence and human possibility is the best we have had so far. That account proposes there is such a thing as "good" and that it is better to be "good" than "bad." Can one imagine Canadian political debate being centred on whether what Canada is doing is "good" or "bad"? This is a hilarious possibility. How would it happen? A morality panel on CBC's *Cross-Country Check-Up*? A ghost-from-the-past *Front Page Challenge* special with the flag as the mystery guest? A David Cronenberg documentary horror film pitting Margaret Atwood against Conrad Black?

That such ideas are the stuff of comedy sketches tells us something about how clearly Grant saw the future course of Canada. Although often accused of being a rhetorician and a polemicist, he was also a supreme realist, the only man of his generation who combined the courage to look unflinchingly into the future and the intellectual power to clearly articulate his vision.

Was my curiosity about George Grant ever satisfied? Did I ever find out what he knew? Yes, in a limited intellectual sense. But finally, no.

What George Grant knew was based on his understanding of classical philosophy and on his Christian faith. Both of these areas are unalterably foreign to me; I could understand his arguments for a while, but I could neither fully inhabit the philosophical assumptions he was working from nor fully empathize with the positions he took as a Christian.

Certainly I realized from the very beginning that these elements existed in his thought. One day, as we walked from his office to his car to go to a restaurant, I brought up the obvious problem that as an egalitarian, he had to believe each person's essential human worth was equal to any other person's, whereas as a Christian he might be encouraged to believe that those who had accepted Christianity were in a different position, in terms of eternity, than others.

It was a November day. We were standing in the parking lot and George Grant had on the dark grey carcoat and scarf that barely contained him. He held out his arms hopelessly. "But I *am* a Christian," he said. "I *am*. I have to believe that Christianity has a higher truth than Judaism or anything else."

In 1971, the Cuban poet and essayist Roberto Fernandez Retamar wrote an essay entitled "Caliban" in which he attempted to defend and define the idea of a Latin American consciousness unique and separate from that of the United States. He relates the story of a European journalist asking him, "Does a Latin-American culture exist?" and goes on to say that such a question might well be expressed as "Do you exist?" because, he says, "To question our culture is to question our very existence, our human reality itself, and thus to be willing to take a stand in favour of our irremediable colonial condition, since it suggests that we would be but a distorted echo of what occurs elsewhere. This elsewhere is of course the metropolis, the colonizing centres, whose 'right wings' have exploited us and whose supposed 'left wings' have pretended and continue to pretend to guide us with pious solicitude—

in both cases with the assistance of local intermediaries of varying persuasions."

That a Cuban and not a Canadian wrote this would not have struck George Grant as peculiar, because Grant, in his view of history, emphasized the importance of empire, and the difference between those at the centre and those on the edges. And seeing the roots of empire as philosophical rather than political, he would also have approved the denunciation of both ends of the political spectrum.

Grant's analysis of empire had much in common with certain Third World analyses of imperialism. But in Canada, his ideas were doubly important because he not only believed in and could articulate our distinct "human reality," he also represented in his own person, history and speech, a walking fragment of the country. No one in Grant's presence could doubt the anxious exuberance of the Canadian reality, the strange way in which English Canada, having gradually peeled off its political diaper in the form of the British flag, was now, quivering and infantile, looking with fear, loathing and desire at the United States.

In *Lament for a Nation* Grant was writing an elegy for a country that never really was, although most certainly the illusion and possibly even the dream had existed. Some of those who read this elegy took it not as a statement of fact, but as a challenge. The generation Grant appealed to in the sixties has now had its chance to come to power. How has Canada fared?

Trudeau's rhetoric of a reinvigorated marriage between French and English Canada is in shreds. So is his vision of a strong national government supported by an amended constitution and renewed east-west economic infrastructure. VIA Rail, the National Energy Policy, the CBC, social services, education: in these and many other areas the actual infrastructure of what used to be Canada has been or is being dismantled. It appears that our government, perhaps in the grip of what some future political Freud will see as a primitive need to sacrifice the first son, has decided to offer our economic and cultural soul to our more powerful neighbour as a gesture of good will.

Has the dream Grant lamented been resurrected even as a voice of opposition? Hardly. If Canada was threatened by integration with the United States thirty years ago, such integration is in many ways now a fact of life. Aside from the North American Free Trade Agreement, and the continuing political integration signalled by our public devotion to the United States, the cultural integration has proceeded apace. From major league sports to the sacrifice of our book and magazine industries, from Wayne Gretzky's emigration to L.A. to the government sellouts of the film industry, from the starvation of the CBC to the use of the board of the Canada Council as a patronage reward, so-called Canadian culture is being gradually transformed into a mosaic of ethnic folk dances to be celebrated by a few people with long memories after they've had a few drinks.

Will we ever wake up from our national amnesia? Our leaders clearly hope not, because the illusion that all is well (Norman Rockwell with a dash of multiracial allspice) is the illusion every Canadian political leader is pledged to maintain. Perhaps what makes us ourselves is, in fact, our collective comfortable sleep. Perhaps the real National Dream is sleep itself, a collective oblivion that we clutch like a child clutches his favourite pillow or stuffed toy.

Anansi

Days

- - - - - - -

drugs and politics exhaust
themselves in writing and then
the move to the country gives me
something to write about
(but is it me? do I care?)

We live in a period when, for better or for worse, most of the realities of writing, publishing and bookselling are being transformed in order to conform to the demands of money. Editorial lists appear and disappear, books are published in enormous quantities with huge promotional campaigns only to be pulped into oblivion, publishing conglomerates come into existence or suddenly vanish. The reason is always the same: money and profit.

Publishing was once considered a "gentlemanly" profession, but the value of a book is now measured only by the number of dollars it represents. Not necessarily through greed, but always by necessity, the measurement of money is applied to every writer, every agent, every publisher. Of course books are still supposed to be good, but "good" is recognized only through sales. Of course many writers still write what they want to write, many agents represent books they believe in, many editors and publishers still bring out books because they like them. Nonetheless, "success" is financial. Even literary prizes are measured not by the merit of the winners but by the size of the prize and its effect on the marketplace.

Is this bad? It could be. Money has taken over publishing not because publishing is a particularly greedy endeavour, or especially vulnerable, but because it has also taken over all other aspects of culture, now known as the entertainment industry. This new order has, of course, displaced the old order, which in Canada was the world of publishing and writing that came into existence at the end of the sixties and beginning of the seventies. Those years were crucial, not because all the best books were written then (they weren't), but because the universe of Canadian literature mutated into a new existence at that time, and has retained approximately the same definition even as it evolved over three decades into something much richer and more unpredictable than its narrow base might have suggested.

That revolution too had a financial aspect. Until the mid-sixties it was considered impossible for a novel published only in Canada to recoup its costs. But then the balance was tipped by a wave of Canadian nationalism—the audience increased, technological changes made typesetting less expensive, and the government began to provide a certain amount of money in the form of support programs for writers and publishers. Within a few years a visible explosion had begun, a burst of energy that transformed CanLit from a curiosity sometimes talked about at Commonwealth conferences into a prominent world literature.

The exact reasons for this trajectory is something to be left to the literary historians, if any exist. For me the transition from being a would-be writer with an imaginary audience of fifty people in downtown Toronto to one who ended up writing for modest but widely scattered audiences that often live in countries about which I know absolutely nothing has not been one I designed, but rather a zigzag, self-contradictory path that has had as many moments of desperation and doubt as times when I could believe I knew what I was doing.

One of these times of complete certainty was while writing my first novel, *Korsoniloff*. I had resolved to work every day because I had spent so many years drifting, and made the surprising discovery that writing itself could be enjoyable. It turned out that sitting in front of a page trying to describe a fingernail or a building or an apparently complex relationship did not involve the deep artistic agony I'd heard so much about. Clack, clack, clack, the typewriter would go. If it was bad, no problem, I just pushed back the carriage and went zxzxzxzx, etc., through the offending sentence or paragraph. In fact zzxxing was incredibly satisfying because I could go so fast and the machine would make such a devastating noise. Then I'd try again. Sometimes the second or third try was so bad I'd have to peer through the zxzxzxzxs to try to decipher what I'd rejected. Eventually, I'd move on. At the end of a day's work I would be sure I had written something that was absolutely astounding (I had the good sense never to reread what I'd done) and perhaps more important, my day's work wouldn't take all day. Far from it! Even though I sometimes stretched the requisite page and a half to two pages or even three, I was generally through in a couple of hours. This would eventually change, but while writing *Korsoniloff* two hours was more than enough for me to discharge what little I had to say, yet sufficiently arduous that I felt I'd renewed my citizenship in the literary micro-universe that was beginning to explode in downtown Toronto.

Through a series of coincidences and random events, I soon found myself at the nexus of what seemed to me three distinct yet attractive ideas of books and publishing, each represented by a publishing house that had carved out its own version of a literary utopia: Anansi Press, the Coach House Press, and McClelland & Stewart.

In the late sixties, with its co-founder Dave Godfrey away in Africa and its eventual co-conspirator Margaret Atwood still in the United States, Anansi was Dennis Lee's to invent and shape. When I first met Dennis he was in his late twenties. Blond, gnomish and nervous, he hid behind a pipe and clouds of smoke, puns and long unfinished sentences, over-brimming with allusions that trailed into the literary distance like a cereal-box series of ever-shrinking footnotes. He had a vaguely pastoral air, which was bizarrely out of place in the freewheeling sixties and seemed intended to set him apart from his petitioners. His most attractive quality, at least from the point of view of his writers and would-be writers, was that he had figured out that the kind of books he was interested in could actually be published without financial ruin. And he had the ability to project such a hypnotically powerful editorial vision onto a manuscript that the writer became convinced that the book he or she was trying to write was the one Dennis had spotted in the midst of the poor supplicant's ill-conceived and clumsily executed mess.

At first I found it hard to understand why Dennis—a Christian, a student of English literature and philosophy, wrapped up in codes of behaviour that seemed to have come from fifties television serials I'd missed—would be interested in an anti-literary semi-barbarian such as myself. On the other hand, he *was* interested in my book, as was I. The book in question was my first and worst novel, *Korsoniloff*, and when one of my characters in "Café Le Dog" said he used to buy up copies of his first book and destroy them, he was very definitely speaking for me.

Nonetheless, despite my own pitiful novel, Anansi was a refreshing and powerful force in the early years of its existence. As a publishing house it was entirely free of the commercial restraints shackling larger houses with more complex infrastructures. It published what it wanted to and didn't depend on foreign publication or approval to make its decisions. Its writers, who included Al Purdy, Margaret Atwood, Michael Ondaatje, George Grant and Dennis Lee himself, were confidently shaping and responding to the wave of Canadian nationalism that had been sweeping the country since Trudeau's election in 1968. Dennis Lee's insistent obsessiveness over detail and vision, combined with Margaret Atwood's genius for understanding and crystallizing the public mood, turned Anansi into a powerhouse of new ideas and new voices—at least within the tiny microcosm that was Canadian literature in the early 1970s.

In 1968 I had moved into an eighteenth-floor apartment in the newly constructed Rochdale College as its first writer-in-residence, an appointment perfectly in tune with Rochdale's open-minded philosophy since I had actually published nothing.

As writer-in-residence-to-be, I was brought to Coach House Press, then as now located on a back alley off Huron

Street just south of Bloor, and introduced to Stan Bevington, Rochdale's official publisher and printer. It turned
out that we had been assigned rooms in the same apartment. Inspecting each other with equally large doses of
suspicion and paranoia, but both aware that these rooms
were absolutely free, we took the news pretty well.

Stan's reputation preceded him: in certain circles of the
late sixties Toronto visual arts and literary scene, Stan was
considered an original and inscrutable genius—enig-
matic, Machiavellian, immune to the pretensions of others and without any himself, so technically adept he was
able to fix and operate anything, so visually astute that his
design ideas were considered incomparable, blessed with
such an original eye that photographs taken by him were
stared at with the dumb worship mere terrestrials reserved
for gifted visitors from outer space.

Stan wasn't from outer space. He came from a small
town in Alberta, where he had apparently invented himself in the basement of the high school of which his father
was the principal.

Even at twenty-five, he was, as they say, ageless. He
had a high-domed forehead that might have belonged
to one of Einstein's seventy-year-old colleagues, close-set
bright-blue eyes that alternately stared and avoided from
behind gold-rimmed glasses, a full red beard and tinges of
grey at the temples. Of average height and very slim, usually dressed in black jeans and a plaid flannel shirt, under
which was usually a T-shirt or even a long-sleeved black
turtleneck, he almost seemed to be leaning backwards,
and moved with a strange anti-physical perfect grace that

just added to the idea he must be entirely ethereal. On that first meeting, when we shook hands, I felt as though I had just agreed to enter into a game whose rules were completely unknown to me and whose point was equally mysterious.

A month later, I moved in. Stan had already installed himself in the room with the clothes cupboard. I, to compensate, had a slightly larger room with a slightly larger window. My furniture was minimal: a mattress, a few boards and enough bricks to separate them into a bookcase, a rug that I had borrowed from the furnace room of a house I'd been living in, a folding chair and—of this item I was extremely proud—a desk, consisting of a gigantic door and two supporting filing cabinets.

The door, of institutional size, glowed with numerous coats of varnish and was only slightly marred by the jagged hole from which the knob had been torn out. This treasure had been found by a saintly friend who had spotted it in a heap of garbage outside Women's College Hospital and had dragged it home with my writing ambitions in mind. The two gun-metal filing cabinets were the contribution of an ex-girlfriend, whose graceful exit from my life had been a relief to both of us (she left to marry a financially secure man who also happened to be, as she said, "the ideal husband and lover").

Drafts of my novel were stacked on the vast expanse of my shining door, its coats of varnish redolent with the texture of the universe and the glorious oeuvre I was planning for myself, and inside the filing cabinets I had stored the short stories I envisioned coming together in a collection that would remind everyone of James Joyce's *Dubliners*, but in an entirely original way.

We were on the highest floor, and although various drug and motorcycle gangs had not yet appropriated the elevators, it still took me several trips to get my furniture, a sound system and a few cardboard boxes of clothes, books and papers into the room.

Stan wasn't there, but the door to his room was ajar and I looked in. It exuded a strange orderliness I took to be his opening move. I unpacked my things. I had no closet or dresser so I put my clothes in my filing cabinets. By the time I was finished, it was dark. I closed my door, locked the apartment behind me and went off to Susie's for dinner.

When I came back the next day, Stan was sitting, perfectly at ease, in the middle of my rug. Carefully arranged around him, in much neater piles than I could have accomplished, were my socks, underwear, T-shirts, etc.

I picked what seemed to be a good space on the rug and sat down. There was no point crossing my legs yoga-style and pretending to go into a trance. Even at twenty-five, I was completely inflexible. For a while we sat there and breathed. The windows faced south, so the place had a nice sunny feeling only slightly overlaid by plaster dust.

"I like your stuff," Stan said. He was looking not at my clothes but at my door desk.

On the door were two bookends from my Aunt Reeva in Israel. She had sent me these bookends after my high-school graduation and I had taken them with me to university, thinking they might be some kind of talisman. But because they were very strangely shaped, I had stuck them in the back of a drawer. Sometimes, when I moved, I considered throwing them out, but I always changed my mind, because it might be bad luck to get rid of something that puzzled me so much. A few moves previously they had ended up in the filing cabinets and been forgotten. Stan, unpacking my belongings, had run across them and now was giving them a good look. The peculiar thing about these bookends was the bizarre angle at which the different pieces of wood had been fitted together. They had a strange inside-out shape that my eyes could never quite get used to, a shape that under the influence of drugs could appear to come from an alternative geometric universe. Stan, possibly aided by the contents of the vials of unmarked pills I later found in the refrigerator door, had entered into this cosmic geometry. Following his example, I settled in and let my eyes turn themselves inside out until the bookends looked entirely normal.

After a while Stan said, "You can put things in the bathroom if you want."

My aunt, who'd gone to live in a Zionist socialist kibbutz in Israel in the late forties, had become a photographer and (it suddenly occurred to me) no doubt possessed that ability to shuffle the visual and spatial deck so common to good artists. Somehow, reading across time, she'd provided me with the only move I'd ever need in the strange game I was or wasn't playing with Stan.

Over the next eighteen years I would publish three books with the Coach House Press, stories in the form of prose poems that I would rewrite dozens of times, each a perfect little physical gem, each designed by Stan with such attention to detail that its merit as an art object was far greater than its slight text.

But text—that repository for all those bothersome and boring words with their predictable insistence on meaning, and their plodding desire to actually articulate it— was only a minor concern for Coach House, which was quickly becoming important both as haven and publishing house for poets, designers and photographers who considered themselves to be working at the edge of (or beyond) anything that could be said or thought.

Victor Coleman was the editor-in-chief and organizing force behind its literary publishing program. This meant not only that he decided what books would be published, but that he maintained ties to West Coast poets such as Robin Blaser, Daphne Marlatt, Frank Davey and George Bowering, as well as a whole American movement of poets and storytellers who ranged from Allen Ginsberg through the Beats to the Black Mountain school of poetry.

I was amazingly ignorant of all this, or almost all of it. I had read the Beat fiction avidly, but I regarded it as an admirable kind of writing firmly placed in the past. But now that I had given myself permission (through Stan) to visit the press whenever I liked, I often spent afternoons at Coach House's upstairs kitchen table, leafing through the amazing variety of chapbooks and small press publications that seemed to arrive by the carton.

The education in aesthetic extremes that I was receiving was sometimes in uncomfortable contrast with the novel I was writing. *Korsoniloff*, despite its avant-garde wardrobe of broken syntax and fragmented construction, was basically an old-fashioned nineteenth-century novel, i.e., a story with a character at the centre.

It could be argued that the most worshipped tradition-breaking book of the century—*Ulysses*—also had character and story. And the same could be said of most of the great Beat writing and the central works of French existentialism by Sartre and Camus. But by the late sixties character and story were precisely the elements of fiction targeted for question and ridicule, and this ridicule would continue to be a theme of most of the new theoretical and literary movements to follow, e.g., post-modernism, semiotics, deconstruction, etc.

Intellectually, I could sympathize. If you want to attack the old, aim for the heart; the whole point of the new aesthetic was, of course, to destroy and replace the old on the grounds that the old no longer represented the world as it was, that the old aesthetic structure merely mirrored the hierarchical political structures responsible for imperialism, gender inequality, racism, the lust for expensive appliances, etc. Also, to the extent that accepting this new aesthetic meant throwing out all the "old" Canadian fiction that had so far been written, I was glad to go along. I hadn't read much of it, but what I had read I'd found stodgy. I wouldn't miss it. Also, getting rid of all the competition in one stroke had its normal attractions.

On the other hand, these theories largely originated with and were being promulgated by tenured university professors, and I was a little sceptical about any arguments they might put forward regarding power. Weren't these advocates of anti-authoritarian revolution in fact the ones who had power and were rapidly accumulating more? And weren't these critics also getting rid of the competition—i.e., the books they used to explicate—in order to replace the so-called traditional texts with their own work?

The nineteenth century, in England, in Russia, in Europe, was still the greatest age of fiction, as far as I was concerned in 1968. True, the trendiest novel of the moment, Gabriel García Márquez's *One Hundred Years of Solitude*, had captured me in a way no other book ever had. It was a great book, but its imitators weren't. What I wanted was not to turn the novel inside out, but instead to find a way to write fiction now that would have the power that fiction had had then. How could I get rid of character and story when my goal was to portray people at the crucial moments of their lives?

The novel I was writing wasn't exactly the fulfilment of these lofty ideas, except theoretically, and I've never trusted theories because they're too easy to invent or tear apart. What I actually had in front of me, despite my desire to peer into the human soul, was a manuscript of about a hundred pages, each one heavily annotated by Dennis Lee.

I was finishing *Korsoniloff* just as Dennis was beginning the final edit on Graeme Gibson's novel *Five Legs*. Dennis, too, was involved in Rochdale—his label was something like "resource person"—and he was also supposed to move in, but his room was unavailable. With my permission (I was spending a lot of my time at Susie's anyway) he moved his editing chair, a giant leather recliner redolent of pipe smoke, into my room for a couple of weeks. Sometimes I would drop in and find the chair surrounded by chapters of Graeme's manuscript. I was curious to see if it was getting the kind of treatment mine was. At first glance the pages seemed equally challenged, with many phrases and sentences entirely struck, others heavily emended. But the comments in the margin were of an entirely different nature. "Great!" "Profound!" "Truly moving!" and other such compliments adorned Graeme's manuscript with the density of stars in a moonless sky. I was shattered. I had spent my life excelling at everything I tried, and now it turned out I had written a novel that was a piece of decorated toilet paper compared to the master-piece that was littering my very own floor: if I had only studied English I would have known whether this was dramatic irony or pathetic fallacy. Thoroughly depressed, I trudged down the eighteen flights of stairs (by now the motorcycle gangs had commandeered the elevators) then slunk down the back lane to Coach House where I breathed deeply of the available drugs and stared into the middle distance of my coffee cup.

A few weeks later I went to Dennis Lee's house to dis-cuss what I had hoped would be the final, or at least penultimate, draft of *Korsoniloff*. By this time the armchair had gone from my room and even the smell of smoke had begun to fade. In the meantime I had asked him about the book he was editing. He mumbled something about it being "a book of great potential," then looked away eva-sively while I enjoyed the feeling of the knife twisting between my ribs. At last Dennis took out my latest draft. Webs of scribbling darkened every page. I began to chal-lenge Dennis's comments, he countered, and soon I was in the ridiculous position of defending, word by word, a book I had already decided was totally lacking.

The problem was, I had no idea how to improve it; I just wanted it to go away. The more Dennis talked, the more I felt invaded by a total and paralysing fatigue. Soon my lymph nodes were aching just the way they'd ached when I'd had mononucleosis a few years before, and then my eyes began to hurt and close of their own accord.

"If you're not interested . . ." Dennis said. "It's your book, after all."

I felt so weighed down I was sure I was going to fall from the chair onto the floor. "I am interested," I said. "I do want to make it better. I just don't understand a word you're saying."

What I meant, of course, was that he wasn't saying the right words. "Great!" "Profound!", etc. Unfortunately those weren't the words he wanted to say. What he wanted, probably, was for me to go home, which I did, dragging my novel as though it were an old dog begging to be put down.

Meanwhile there was life at Rochdale.

Before it even opened, Rochdale had been occupied by the city's teenage foot soldiers of the psychedelic revolution. To cynics like me it seemed clear that this so-called revolution had evolved into a series of financial opportunities for the unscrupulous, but I was in a minority. Certainly those running Rochdale, young hairy dope-smoking idealists who believed they could combine business acumen with cutting-edge trendiness—failed rock promoters, I used to call them, but no one was listening—weren't going to soil their credentials by calling in the police to remove these nonpaying guests. Nor was anyone else. A symbiotic co-existence developed between the few hundred actual legitimate university students, who justified Rochdale's mortgage status as an educational institution by renting rooms there in a normal way, and the equal number of crashers who occupied the corridors, the dining halls and dozens of unfinished rooms and suites. There were other non-rent-paying occupants, who were exempted because they were artists who'd been invited, dope dealers too scary to ask for rent, professors who were supposed to be educational role models and supervisors, Americans who were coming to Canada either to escape the draft or as a protest against American imperialist policies in Vietnam and elsewhere, and miscellaneous opportunists who simply moved in and installed bolts and chains on their doors.

In sum, the place had the scrambled ambience of an ocean liner that had been sinking for several months.

Among the so-called artists in residence was my old friend Tamio Wakayama. His relationship with his girlfriend had been falling apart for a year, and when I told him about the situation I was going to enjoy at Rochdale, he went to work on his own behalf. Already familiar with Coach House (which had published a brilliant book of his photographs, a book that had received enough international notice that Tamio's limitless confidence in his own abilities seemed justified), he decided to negotiate a deal for himself. He ended up not with one of two rooms in a small apartment, but with a huge suite—two bedrooms plus living room plus dining room plus kitchen, all to himself.

In his living room, pretty well devoid of furniture except for a giant shag rug he must have purchased from a *Playboy* fantasy, and an outrageously expensive sound system he'd bought with the profits from some other unspeakable boondoggle, we would often spend half the night listening to Bob Dylan and drifting along on the tide of whatever drug had happened to be available.

It was a time of rapid swings from manic energy to depressed emptiness. Both of us had been captured, then abandoned by the political currents of the sixties. The nonviolence movement and the struggle against racism and segregation had been subsumed into a broader power struggle under the pressure of the Vietnam War. Of course I opposed the war, supported and admired those Americans who opposed it, and was happy to participate in demonstrations and marches against it. But the utopian idealism of the early sixties had been replaced by the reality of a power struggle between the American centre left on the one hand, and the so-called "military-industrial complex" and its political allies on the other. The assassination of Martin Luther King was not only a terrible and tragic attack on a great human being, it was also a signal that the consensus and ideals he stood for had no place in a struggle whose two sides were becoming so polarized they had begun to bear an unpleasant resemblance to each other.

Nor was the new psychedelic movement a substitute for the old political idealism; at least not for me. Drugs were an amusing and sometimes transforming essential but—aside from the fact that they and the music, clothes, etc., they were associated with had become commercialized—the alternative world they offered rang false to me. Living in Rochdale, how could I think otherwise? Dozens, even hundreds of wired adolescents wandered the building and rode the elevators day and night, their pimpled faces, shaking limbs, pinpoint-pupilled eyes broadcasting the exact details of their speed habits. They weren't blowing their minds, they were just scrambling their brains. So was I, perhaps, but it was different for me: true, I was stupid and self-destructive at times, but I also had a sense of self-preservation. I was using drugs, yes, but they were being used by drugs.

Or so I reassured myself at the time. Eventually I came to realize the obvious: that everyone thinks they are in charge of their drugs. Everyone thinks they take drugs to be empowered, not to be reduced. In any case, the drugs revolution never convinced me. As with the anti-war marches, I was happy to participate, but I didn't have the visceral sense that the world was about to be transformed.

Nonetheless, there we were, jaded politicos and not-quite hippies inhabiting a building that was a real estate scam disguised as educational idealism. Sitting in Tamio's living room, drinking green tea and looking out his window to Bloor Street, I couldn't help thinking how absurd it was that having somehow exhausted the revolutionary politics of my generation, I had ended up choosing something as inherently conservative as literature as a way out. Literature, it turned out, would agree.

Korsoniloff was one of five novels published by Anansi on the same day. Anansi had already published some fiction, notably Graeme Gibson's *Five Legs*, which received a

critical welcome almost equal to Dennis's editorial enthusiasm. But with the simultaneous publication of five first
novels Anansi was making a statement about the existence
of a whole wave of new writing. Probably the best of the
five were *Fallout*, by Peter Such, who went on to write several more books, and *The Telephone Pole*, by Russell
Marois, who committed suicide a few years later by
throwing himself in front of a train. Just before the official
publication date, we were asked to appear on CBC-Radio,
to be interviewed by William French, then the *Globe and
Mail*'s book columnist and a powerful figure on the literary scene who was more inclined to diffident ambiguity
than high praise or extreme disapproval. Thus it was that
four trembling first-novelists (the Québécois writer,
Pierre Gravel, was unable to come) duly sat around a table
covered with velvet to deaden the sound of dropping pen-
cils or falling tears, while at its head William French prepared to interview us. The first thing he did was to hand
out pre-publication copies of his review. I was so nervous I
could hardly read it, but the drift was clear: *The Telephone
Pole* had been singled out for approval, and the rest were
quite gently dismissed as worthy efforts.

I'd had my own reservations about my novel, but I'd
also put a tremendous amount of work and hope into it,
including the hope that others would somehow see gold
where I feared there was only lead. Now, in a couple of
sentences my eyes were almost too blurred to read, the
worst had been confirmed. While the interview proceeded, I slowly deflated. So, this was getting published. It
reminded me of an unpleasant visit to the dentist's office.
When the interview was over, I went with the others for a

beer. I don't know what they were thinking, but I was burning with the desire to go home and get back to work on a project I had already started—one that now had a new burden, that of rescuing my name and my reputation, especially my reputation with myself.

Although by the standards of Rochdale College and the Coach House Press I was an aesthetic Neanderthal, I had formed an idea of myself as an experimental small-press writer. Perhaps in order to justify myself in terms of childhood expectations, I had come to see fiction as almost a science: something to be done both for its own sake and in order to better understand the world, an activity as susceptible to amelioration and progress as was the search for a new vaccine or a superior understanding of the laws of matter.

But I couldn't help remembering that I had already given up on being a scientist. And that the whole idea of progress was one about which I had become very sceptical. So I went the next step and decided that for me writing didn't have to be boringly systematic. I could just imagine myself as a classically trained jazz musician, using a traditional base from which to improvise the new riffs that would render, faithfully but not *literally*, all those new lives and feelings.

For a charter member of the drug generation nothing could have been more perfect. I would be, I decided, a new model Beat (an orientation that no one except two of my translators has ever noticed), a psychedelic classicist Jack Kerouac who had substituted marijuana and LSD for speed, Flaubert and Camus for Balzac and Victor Hugo. I began writing a novel, eventually called *Johnny Crackle Sings*, that would be a set of hallucinatory images somehow illuminating the consciousness of my generation by using the iconography of rock music as a mythic counterpoint.

What a great idea! I busily began hallucinating and writing down fragments of whatever came into my mind. If this wasn't the future of world literature, could literature hope to have a future?

On another level, I knew I was writing this book because of the disaster of *Korsoniloff*. Though the reviews that followed William French's were mostly "respectful," I myself continued to loathe both the novel and its author. I needed to vindicate myself. Not to the public I didn't have or the reviewers I was hardly aware of, but to myself. It wasn't that I wanted to "become a writer." That was not an ambition, but something I fell into by default. I just wanted to write one incredible world-transforming book and then retire with my honour intact and my hands clean.

If *Korsoniloff* had been intended to provide a fictional mirror for the fragmentation of reality, *Johnny Crackle Sings* was a kaleidoscope made up of a set of mirrors on which I'd dropped a large rock. Unfortunately, I had no idea what the mirrors had been before I broke them. Writing the little bits of glass was easy enough—the problem was finding a way to assemble them. I had read the story of how Thomas Wolfe had brought his manuscripts to the famous Scribner's editor, Maxwell Perkins, in a cardboard box. Perkins had then taken out the randomly offered pages, rewritten and assembled them, then given America a masterpiece with Thomas Wolfe's name on it.

To me, this seemed an entirely reasonable author/ editor division of labour. The genius was surely in the conception of the book, the original Big Bang on which everything else depended, the feverish days and nights spent hunched over the typewriter. Setting the whole mess in order was, when you thought about it carefully, essentially a janitorial task best left to those with expertise in such matters and the plodding patience belonging to those unsinged by inspiration. All I needed was to find someone who both understood this role and was capable of playing it.

I first considered Coach House Press because I knew they would probably publish anything I wrote, and that the book would look exquisite. The problem was the editor, Victor Coleman. Brilliant, precocious, egotistical, Victor was not about to play second fiddle to his authors. Not that he hesitated to collaborate in the writing—on the contrary. I even participated in various collaborative writing exercises with him and other Coach House poets. These sessions were invariably amusing and educational, but in the end I always felt as though I'd just been a part of a gymnastic meet and was lying exhausted on the floor while Victor was still effortlessly doing back flips. I admired his ability, but my only model being the editorial experience I'd had with Dennis on *Korsoniloff*, couldn't imagine surviving a similar process with Victor. And yet I believed my manuscript desperately needed someone other than me. It would take a long time to learn that only the writer can realize his or her own book. Perhaps I only fully accepted the lesson after I had switched roles a few times and become, temporarily, an editor and teacher.

Editors can do a lot to improve a manuscript, but despite what one reads in the acknowledgements and dedications, editors can't point the way when there is none.

And so I went back to the devil I knew, Dennis Lee and Anansi. After all, publishers were supposed to stick by their writers. Also, Dennis had become very involved with George Grant through the editing of *Technology and Empire*. Sometimes in this process I'd been able to be helpful, and I felt that the link with Grant, and the continuity that link provided in my own life, meant that the strategy of staying with Anansi was the right one. I began showing parts of *Johnny Crackle Sings* to Dennis. He expressed enough enthusiasm that I showed him more. Gradually the frosty aftermath of *Korsoniloff* melted away and I began to believe that Anansi had taken on the new novel.

Understandably (though I didn't understand) Anansi had its own point of view. Presented with early drafts of *Johnny Crackle Sings*, they hemmed and hawed until what had once been friendly welcoming faces froze into grotesque icy gorgons.

Finally, after (or so I thought) repeatedly assuring me they would publish the book, though there had never been anything in writing, they sent me an actual letter. It was signed by Dennis, and stated that on the advice of several readers and his partner, Dave Godfrey, Anansi was turning down *Johnny Crackle*. As Godfrey had already started a new publishing house, New Press, and it was impossible for me to imagine Dennis acceding to any judgement but his own, I took his letter not as a measure of the quality of my book (which I knew to be a mess in search of salvation) but as a deliberate and malicious betrayal. It obsessed me totally and though I blamed everything but the book itself, every time I opened the manuscript I found it full of flaws and rewrote furiously, trying to efface whatever it was that was holding it back. I would work on it for hours every day, blindly rewriting and restructuring. I wasn't seeking publication at this point: what I was trying to do was shake the kaleidoscope until the right picture emerged.

During the year I lived in Rochdale, my rent-free status and savings from McMaster took care of my financial needs. But when I left Rochdale to live with Susie it became clear that I was going to have to earn money. My first, though least reasonable, hope—and even thirty years and twenty books have not prevented me from nurturing this insane hope with every one of my publications since—was that the publication of *Korsoniloff* would bring me a lifetime of financial security. There was one particular day I was absolutely certain my ship had come in. I had telephoned Anansi to say I would be dropping around to pick something up and Shirley Gibson, the managing editor of Anansi and Graeme Gibson's wife, told me not to come that afternoon because she would be "busy with film people." Something mysterious and seductive in her voice gave away the secret she was obviously trying to keep: someone from Hollywood was about to purchase the rights to *Korsoniloff*, but she hadn't wanted to say anything until the deal was complete.

That afternoon, wearing a pair of clip-on sunglasses to disguise myself, I spent over an hour casually lurking around across the street, observing the comings and goings. Sure enough, around two o'clock an attaché case came to the house where Anansi was located. I waited a little while longer, then hurried back to Susie's and prepared for the telephone to ring. The idea that Hollywood might come knocking for a first novel by an unknown writer was even more unlikely then than now. However, even then Toronto was the centre of a certain amount of film activity, and someone claimed to have seen Peter O'Toole on a nearby street. Suppose he had dropped into a bookstore and, purely by chance, picked up my book. Suppose he had seen the picture of the bearded young swashbuckler I then was and said to himself (actors are renowned for their vanity) that no matter how handsome and sensitive the author had contrived to make himself appear, he, Peter O'Toole, world-famous actor, ladies' man and all-round sport, was even better looking and more sensitive. Suppose in this mood of playful competitiveness, he had actually opened the book and had been drawn in by the story of Korsoniloff himself, that ambiguously indecisive existential shadow, knifing his way through the darkness of life like, for example, Lawrence of Arabia slicing through the desert night.

A few days later I mustered the courage to call Shirley and ask her, incidentally as it were, what had happened with the film people. "Ah, yes," she said, her voice snapping into focus, "I do think they're quite serious. We did talk about a contract." How much? I wanted to ask, but managed to restrain myself.

"But," she continued, "I don't know if they're right for the book. Really, it's up to Graeme."

Graeme? I almost blurted, as an entirely unwanted realization had occurred.

"I always thought Graeme's book would make a great movie," I said.

"So does everyone," Shirley agreed. "It's just a matter of settling on the right buyer."

In fact Graeme did end up getting some sort of a deal to write a script and even without my reminding him that his novel had been edited in my room, he generously shared his wealth by offering me many a drink in many a bar (we didn't yet know *my* novel had been partially written in *his* room) so I did in fact receive a benefit from the world of film. Nonetheless, I still needed to make a living, and given that *Korsoniloff* was going to neither sell copies nor be a vehicle for Peter O'Toole, I turned my attention to two of the guardians of Toronto's closed literary gates: Robert Fulford and Robert Weaver.

These two men, sometimes known as the Two Bobs, were the kingpins of a small empire that included *Saturday Night* magazine, CBC-Radio's *Anthology* series (then Canada's best market for short stories), CBC-Radio drama and *The Tamarack Review* (then Canada's most influential literary magazine). In addition, both appeared on various CBC cultural programs, and both were influential newspaper and magazine reviewers; before taking over *Saturday Night*, Robert Fulford had been books editor at *The Toronto Star* for several years. The Two Bobs, along with William French, who in addition to being book editor at *The Globe and Mail* was a regular contributor to CBC-Radio, made up a terrifying triumvirate, who, at least in Toronto, appeared to have gathered unto themselves the exclusive power to make or break a writer's reputation. They were also white, middle-aged, middle-class conservatives who did not appear (though of course appearances can be deceiving) to have decided to sacrifice their lives to the untrammelled hedonism of the sixties; on the contrary, they appeared to be quite happy as 1950s reactionaries.

From the outside it also looked as though the three had conspired to preserve their power by coming to unanimous decisions: like a triumvirate of Roman consuls they occupied the tribunal whenever a new writer was so foolish as to enter the ring. While shapeless minor beasts in the form of secondary reviewers and cynical bookstore owners bared their tobacco-stained teeth and broke the heads off a few Scotch bottles in order to tear the foolish candidate to shreds, the three consuls watched from on high, noses carefully pinched, and disdainfully flipped through the pages of the day's offering. Thumbs down and the foolish aspirant was reduced to an instant remainder, a clause in a sentence in an annual review of the year's books—which would read something like ". . . and also, among the first novels, a confused but not entirely unsuccessful attempt to satirize the university; of equal interest was a woman's novel in the form of a dialogue between two nameless . . ."

In fact my debut had been only mildly disastrous. William French had actually mentioned it in his column, and had I not been so thin-skinned I might not have scissored his comments to bits and set them on fire in an ashtray. Robert Fulford had refrained from mentioning *Korsoniloff* at all. A minor West Coast counterbalance to the triumvirate, the not at all terrifying George Woodcock, had given it a positive notice. In sum, it seemed to me that fate had decided I was so young that it would be better to allow a second book before the definitive annihilation.

In this optimistic mood I contacted *Saturday Night* and proposed an article about the Coach House Press. My hope was that by writing for a magazine with glossy covers I might gain an audience and also receive a cheque. In addition, it seemed to me absurd that while small presses such as Coach House were producing a wide variety of interesting work, their books went virtually unmentioned in the mainstream media. Shortly afterwards I was invited to meet Robert Fulford in person, at his office. Nervous, I showed up at the appointed time, full of carefully rehearsed rationalizations for my article and carrying a bundle of Coach House books under my arm.

Invited to sit down, I put my books on the desk between us and watched as Fulford picked them up and leafed through them without enthusiasm. Fulford was not at that time known as a friend to the new Canadian writing. His admiration for certain established Canadian writers was well balanced by public scepticism about young university intellectuals—Fulford, himself, as he often mentioned, was an autodidact who had never been to university. As he set the books down without comment, I began to feel as though I were some kind of horrible traitor for trying to exchange my knowledge about Coach House for mere money. I began to realize there were good reasons why places like Coach House didn't bother to court the media. I was not only a traitor, but an idiot.

"Isn't Victor Coleman the editor at Coach House Press?" Fulford asked me.

I nodded.

"Who ever told him he could be a writer?"

In the end my idea for an article was reduced to a modest review with an introductory paragraph about the press. And when I submitted the review, a second meeting took place, during which Fulford gave me some excellent and necessary advice about writing comprehensibly for people who had no knowledge of my subject.

But what stuck was his question about Victor Coleman: *Who ever told him he could be a writer?* Implicit in this question was the reality of the Canadian writing scene—one very powerful man's idea of the rules of the game.

1. Being "a writer" was a sociological status conferred by others, not by one's own drive, desires or talents.

2. This meant that there was no such thing as "talent," which, if it existed, would presumably belong to the would-be author. Instead there was "taste," i.e., the ability to declare what was good and what was bad. "Taste" belonged not to writers but to critics. How convenient for the critics.

3. The consuls must be courted and won over. *Who ever told him he could be a writer?* implied that only certain people got to confer this exalted status. This select group, from whom the only effective appeal was either bestsellerdom or the even more exalted rulers in the imperial centres of London or New York, weren't at all eager to have their status-conferring powers shared around. An upstart critic would doubtless receive the same treatment as an upstart writer. Particularly annoying was the idea that some place like the Coach House

Press could simply set itself up by purchasing a printing press, then publishing whatever it wanted and selling the unauthorized result to its doubtlessly drugged and insensate friends and followers without even attempting to gain the approval of the consuls. Other publishers—from the established, like M&S or Macmillan, to the new, like Anansi—had the decency to attempt to flatter, wine and dine. This was the established way, though of course such methods could not guarantee success. Coach House Press, like some others who were insane enough to attempt publishing independence by setting up in other cities or even faraway provinces, deserved the treatment they got, the most feared scourge the empire had to offer: ostracism.

I now realized that the reason my proposal had been accepted, albeit in reduced and shrunken form, was that by humbly presenting myself and my idea, I had recognized and obeyed the reality of the literary power structure.

Of course, having seen how the land lay—at least through the paranoid's window—I could have decided to imitate the Coach House Press, completely withdraw and refuse to have anything to do with any kind of literary society. In this splendid isolation I could have produced works of genius completely uncorrupted by any outside influence. The problem was that although I thought the idea of cultural czars deciding what was "literature" was ridiculous, I was equally sceptical of the solitary-genius idea. Language, after all, is something we have all invented together. In spite of the fact that we constantly misunderstand each other, it is what human beings have in common. Also, or so I think, any given piece of writing is a common endeavour. I may set down a certain sentence, but how that sentence rings and resonates, the allusions it calls forth, the universe it brings into existence, depends as much on the reader as on me. All books are cooperative works-in-progress between writer and reader—but especially fiction, which depends on the reader agreeing to be brought into the world the writer is trying to suggest.

Although I'd retreated from politics I still wanted to influence the world around me. I was less worried about writing so-called great literature (a label I thought to be the property of people so different from me that they couldn't possibly be interested in my books) than in writing books that would have a voice in my own country's culture and consciousness. Anyone with such thoughts today would probably go into television or movies. But when I was growing up in the fifties and sixties, books had a weight now impossible to imagine, and though more far-sighted people may have foreseen their collapse, I didn't.

My first meeting with Robert Weaver took place in the café of the Four Seasons Hotel, across the street from the old CBC building on Jarvis Street north of Carlton. He said I would recognize him by the fact that he would be wearing a tweed jacket and smoking a pipe. When I arrived at the café entrance at eleven in the morning, I saw a man answering Weaver's self-description sitting across from a young woman I took to be another supplicant. He was in the midst of lighting his pipe—a gesture he repeated about a hundred times an hour—and in the same motion he recognized me and gave a wave that I translated as, "Don't worry, your turn will come."

When the chair opposite him was empty, Weaver signalled me to come over. As I approached he took off his glasses and prepared to shake hands. In his uniform of tweed jacket, grey flannels, white shirt and tie, with his ready smile and a panoply of nervous tics and gestures, he seemed like a cross between an Ottawa civil servant and a self-invented, self-conscious secret agent from a British spy novel no one else had read.

When the waiter came over Weaver ordered what I later learned must have been his tenth coffee of the morning, glanced at me, then took a pile of manuscripts in tattered brown envelopes from the chair beside him and gave them a series of rapid little pats. My own brown envelope, in which I'd sent my latest submissions for *Anthology*, was on top. Having only previously had editorial discussions with Dennis Lee, I presumed that Weaver was about to take the stories and dissect them word by word. Instead, after patting them, he returned the envelopes to the chair and reached into his jacket for a fresh pipe.

He then began telling me a long story about one of his monthly lunches with Morley Callaghan—"You know Morley Callaghan, don't you?"—during which he'd had to admonish Callaghan, saying, "But Morley, surely you didn't think Ernest Hemingway was going to like you for punching him in the nose," or "But Morley, I can't have one of your stories on every one of my programs, people will think it's the *Morley Callaghan Show*."

Meanwhile, underneath my denim jacket, which it was now too late to remove, I was sweating buckets. Why was he so proud of having lunch with Morley Callaghan every month? What did he think of my stories and was he going to buy one? If I punched someone in the nose would he think more of me? I could tell him about the time I stood up for my brother but it never seemed to be my turn to talk. Suddenly Weaver was re-relighting his pipe and waving to someone at the entrance of the café. It was time for me to leave. He pulled the brown envelope from the chair and patted it again before extracting the two stories. One was what I considered a hilariously comic parody of heavy Russian melodrama; the other was a plodding imitation of the kind of story I sometimes read in *Saturday Night* or *Chatelaine*. It was the blow-by-blow account of an affair I wished I'd had. He tapped this second one. "There's something very fresh about this. I'd like to take it. You should be getting a contract in a week or two."

I've never considered myself an infallible judge of my own work. During the long-drawn-out, often frustrating process of revision, there are thousands of small decisions to be made, but for me the purpose of these subtractions and additions and reshufflings is to make whatever it is a more perfect example of itself. But to judge the idea as a whole is fatal. It's true that for some stories, and even novels, the only revision I've been able to think of was to throw the whole thing out. Most of the time that was doubtless the right decision, though one novel I wanted to throw out was *Elizabeth and After*, which only my editor saved from oblivion, and though in the long run it will probably find that very destination, it seems to have been my most successful novel.

I was amazed that for years Robert Weaver, the most eclectic of the consular triumvirate, invariably picked my most boring stories and rejected what I considered to be the best ones as self-indulgent and excessive. Perhaps while feeding coffee to some other eager neophyte, or even at his monthly lunch with Morley Callaghan, he would recount his responses to my complaints: "But Matt, if you could choose among your own stories you'd have been an editor, not a writer," or "Matt, I told him, you may have your reasons for liking this story but you wouldn't want me to be dishonest with you." After a few years, inexplicably, our taste in my stories began to converge. Meanwhile our annual coffee-meetings became so friendly that I began to feel—although I'd never met him—that I myself was having monthly lunches with Morley Callaghan.

In the spring of 1970, Susie and I moved to a farm north of Kingston. Since neither of us had a job or any prospect of one, our decision was not so strange as it might seem today. In fact, at the time, moving to the country was a serious option for one-time sixties pacifist idealists who had watched left-wing politics dissolve into the drug culture, gender wars, various guerrilla and terrorist groups, etc. If one couldn't save the world one could at least save oneself.

I'm not sure we thought we were saving ourselves, but at least from my point of view the move was desirable. Since my resignation from McMaster, I had spent a lot of time driving about the continent in my red Volkswagen. There had been not only the trips to Golden in British Columbia and Terrence Bay in Nova Scotia, but a long triangular peregrination that had taken me and Susie from Toronto to Vancouver, on to various West Coast communities and islands, then down the coast to see old Toronto friends who now lived right in the heart of the

Haight-Ashbury district of San Francisco. We'd returned to Toronto by driving across the United States
and spent much of the following fall at Susie's mother's
cottage on Lake Huron.

Ever since I'd arrived in Toronto in the fall of 1960, I
had been sinking deeper and deeper roots into the culture
of the big city. I adored the buzz of it, the endless variety,
the smoky grit of Toronto summers and the dirty slushy
winters. Fume-belching buses, crowded subways, the
packed malodorous corridors of Honest Ed's—all these
had entranced me after a youth spent in Ottawa.

But now came the rip tide. The mountains, the coasts,
the wonderful vastness of the Prairies, the sea, the ancient
hieroglyphic splendour of the Great Lakes . . . The woods,
the hills, the winding roads that led deeper and deeper into
landscapes apparently utterly unconnected with downtowns
and pavement. The wonder of clean air in my lungs, lakewa-
ter or ocean on my body, the possibility of seeing sunrises
and sunsets in a distance farther away than the houses across
the street or the office buildings along University Avenue.

Even the ingrown community of Toronto literary culture that had once so attracted and amused me now began
to repel and bore. How I had loved the fact I could go to
certain bars and cheap restaurants and be sure to run into
someone I knew, someone also enslaved to the typewriter.
Almost every day I had made the rounds of my tiny literary universe, dropping in at Coach House to have a coffee
in the kitchen, passing by Anansi to hear the gossip about
the latest literary sensation.

Now it seemed to me that every street corner was in-
fested with people trying to turn themselves into novelists

and poets. Having had my own first novel published didn't help. On the contrary. Now I had traded in my protean and anonymous ambition to write the perfect piece of fiction, with all the infinite possibility that implied, for the disgraceful reality of being responsible for an actual book whose very finite limitations had been a matter of public comment. Being a published author, it turned out, was the modern equivalent of being displayed in stocks.

The farm was in Frontenac County, a narrow jagged rectangle of rocky Shield, swamps and lakes that begins at Kingston and stretches north well past Highway 7. I, the self-proclaimed rootless Jew, was incredibly pleased to be moving back to the county of my birth, to be claiming my heritage in the midst of this hilly and rock-strewn land so useless for farming as to be virtually worthless. But there was a lot of it—over four hundred acres of pine and maple and marsh that I instantly fell in love with.

The farm had a small, standard-issue, one-and-half-storey white frame house with wooden siding, and enough barns and outbuildings to house thirty cattle, a few horses and a dozen pigs.

The house was entirely unspoiled by renovation. The kitchen featured simplicity: a small sink with a drain that led out the back wall. The well with its hand pump was on the front lawn beneath a giant maple, the bathroom was a wooden outhouse placed over a pit best left undescribed. All furnishings, including the kitchen stove, had been removed, but down in the basement was a giant wood furnace, a pre-electric fan model in the shape of an octopus with its huge swollen tentacles reaching out to the various hot-air registers on the ground floor. Second-storey heat was provided by the stairwell and a tin stove pipe, which in order to distribute its heat zigged and zagged through the house, joints dripping creosote, until finally meeting up with a brick chimney in the main bedroom.

The first night was freezing cold. First thing the next morning I went downstairs and, using my trusty axe, some wood that had been left behind and a couple of newspapers, started a fire. Smoke had been pouring out the windows of the house for about half an hour when a passing neighbour came up the driveway to investigate. With his help we carried in buckets of water from the well, doused the fire in the furnace, then climbed up on the roof and removed the starling nest from the chimney.

That afternoon I found a broken old handmower in the pig barn. I dragged it out to the front lawn, thinking that if I oiled and sharpened the blades, it might be the solution to our lawnmowing problems. I was just sitting and admiring the work I was about to do when the neighbour from across the road came to introduce himself. When I explained my project to him he nodded sagely and rolled himself a cigarette. A couple of weeks later, when the grass had grown and I'd torn my hands to shreds trying to operate the useless antique, I woke up one morning to a loud roar outside the bedroom window. Rushing downstairs I saw that the neighbour's sixteen-year-old son was taking care of our lawn with a large power mower. Pride told me to step outside and stop him. But if I had listened to pride I would never have become a writer. Instead I went back to bed and pretended to be asleep.

Even the dog neighbours were alarmed at our incompetence. First a black Labrador from up the road came to investigate a couple of times. Then, the day after our grass had been mowed, I woke up to find a black-and-white collie sleeping picturesquely in the centre of the lawn. When I went outside he licked my hand as though we'd been meeting this way for years, then followed me around as I made my tour of the barns and the outhouse. Sometime during the afternoon he disappeared, but the next morning he was on the lawn again, happily asleep in the sun.

A few days later the neighbour from down the road drove up and explained that our new lawn ornament was in fact his prized Border collie, a trained cow herder who had actually been to school and who earned his keep by bringing in the cattle every afternoon for milking. Something in the way he said this made me know he was wondering how it was I earned my keep.

In fact, the community Susie and I had moved into had not previously experienced the arrival of urban misfits, and it turned out that the natural reaction of both dogs and neighbours was to try to make us one of their own. Until just a few years ago, when the advent of chainsaws and powerful tractors ended the custom, such activities as woodcutting and haying had been carried out communally, the men going from farm to farm until all the work was done. Now, over the next few weeks, I was sold an old tractor from someone's barn, taken to the chainsaw store, and offered various suggestions about how our land could be kept in production for modest rents—all this in the hope that I might add up to something.

At the same time, I was busily trying to renovate the house. I had no idea what I was doing but fortunately Richard Oughton, an ex-city friend who now lived in a nearby village and knew how to do everything, generously volunteered to spend a few weekends showing me the miracles of plumbing and wiring. The red Volkswagen got traded for a shiny half-ton truck, and soon I was driving about with loads of copper tubing and two-by-fours. To receive the eventual gifts of our new technology, a septic tank had been installed. Also, the bug season had commenced in earnest and trips to the outhouse were a race for survival. Finishing the plumbing changed from a hobby to a serious emergency. The Saturday Richard was supposed to help me connect the bathroom and the kitchen to the well pump, he forgot to come. Thinking this must be a lesson in self-reliance, and unable to face another week of sharing my flesh with mosquitoes and horseflies, I decided to do it myself. In a manic burst of activity I plumbed the entire house in an afternoon. I was feeling so energetic when I finished that I decided to cap the whirlwind of activity by building a set of bookcases for the room I had elected to be my study.

Sunday, Richard and his wife showed up. She was pregnant and feeling nauseous, so lay down in the living room. Proudly I pointed out the wonderful structure of copper pipes snaking through the living room on their way from the bathroom to the water pump, then took Richard down to the basement to show him the rest.

"Why don't we try it out?" he asked.

"Turn it on?"

"Yeah." He flicked the switch of the pump. There was the smooth sound of water gushing into the pipes from a brand new Canadian Tire jet pump, then a loud scream from the room above us. I went running upstairs to discover

Richard's wife cowering in the corner as water gushed from every one of the joints I had so expertly soldered. As we spent the next few hours taking apart and redoing all my handiwork, I was able to console myself that at least I had cut the copper tubing to the correct length.

As an additional prize, I had the bookcase I'd constructed with my surplus energy. When Stan Bevington came to the visit the farm, he looked at it appraisingly, and judged it "a jigsaw puzzle put together by a madman." This was the only compliment I ever received from him. Seeing me in my rural splendour must have thrown him into a sentimental mood.

When I started writing after resigning from McMaster, I had promised myself I would produce at least a page and a half a day. But once I had my varnished door installed in my rural study with its madman's bookcase and my historic army filing cabinets, the relative diffidence with which I'd approached trying to write quickly evolved into an all-consuming anxiety. Part of this evolution was due to the obvious: writing and publishing books like *Korsoniloff* wasn't exactly my idea of what I wanted to do with my life. *Johnny Crackle Sings* seemed better to me, but was still far too slight a project to contain my ballooning ambition to capture the whole world in fiction.

On the one hand I thought I knew where such overblown ambitions led: to equally overblown novels, gigantesque self-inflated disasters. On the other hand I needed to do something more than the technically experimental fiction I'd been trying. I wanted to dig into people, dig into their hearts and their souls and their darkest, most convoluted secrets. Yet no matter how many hours I spent at my desk, I couldn't seem to break through the surface.

Then the unexpected happened: through a series of coincidences and intrusions, an Ottawa friend of the family got the manuscript of *Johnny Crackle Sings* to McClelland & Stewart. Soon after, a rumour reached me that Canada's least hip, most tasteless and most commercial (this was from the Coach House and Anansi point of view, which I had been cultivating) but also most powerful and prestigious publishing house was interested in publishing my novel.

Eventually an actual letter arrived, an ambiguous statement of interest and possible intent that I took as the prelude to an offer to publish. The letter was signed by the executive editor of McClelland & Stewart, Anna Szigethy, who later became Anna Porter. After studying it carefully, I called her on the telephone. A woman with a dry Eastern European accent answered: I pictured a sixty-five-year-old dragon lady with the hawkish features of my first violin teacher.

A few weeks later, clutching this document that was neither acceptance nor rejection, I kicked the cow shit off my work boots, got into my red Mazda truck and drove from the farm to Toronto to face the dragon in person.

The drive was the most nerve-racking of my life. My gut was a black anxious pit into which, all along the two-hour stretch of 401 that joins Kingston to Toronto, I kept stopping to pour more cups of black coffee. On the seat beside me I had the letter. Every time I read it, it became clearer to me that what they'd sent was not the expression of a desire to publish me, but a brush-off. Nonetheless, I'd somehow gotten myself an appointment with this so-called executive editor and obviously my only hope was to beg for mercy, promise a few thousand more revisions and charm her with my then plentiful curls and utterly fake boyish helplessness.

One thing of which I was certain: if the M&S axe did fall, I was finished professionally. By not giving my manuscript to Coach House I had burned my bridges there. The fight I'd had with Anansi had been accompanied by the kind of intemperate comments a man can't help admiring as he's making them. If I had to climb back into my red Mazda and drive home without a contract, I was going to have to learn to be a real farmer, which involved far too much physical labour, or get down on my hands and knees and ask McMaster to take me back, which would be a terrible admission of defeat and worse, would necessitate my returning to graduate school to finish my Ph.D.

The fabled and vilified McClelland & Stewart was located not in some suitably historic downtown architectural masterpiece but in a huge warehouse-style structure plunked in the middle of a suburb whose name I would never learn. It was impressive only in its large anonymous absurdity, and as I parked my truck and checked my hair in the rear-view mirror I wondered what kind of publisher could choose such an anti-heroic setting. Inside I found someone to give me directions, and was immediately shown into Anna's office. I assumed the woman behind the desk, someone my own age, was her secretary.

It's fair to say there are certain things of which I wasn't aware. For example, that the smell of cow dung, which outlasts its actual physical presence, would be remarkably out of place even in the modest Hollinger Road offices of M&S. Or that Anna Szigethy would not be a recycled violin teacher but a twenty-five-year-old long-haired Hungarian blonde sophisticate who would find it strange that an author would wear the clothes I was wearing and sit in her office dribbling tobacco on the floor as he nervously hand-rolled cigarettes while waiting for the axe to fall.

I also couldn't have guessed Anna Szigethy's complete distance from that circle of Canadian publishing that to me had become the whole literary universe. Her family had become refugees after the Second World War; they had moved first from Hungary to Australia, where she grew up, then to London where she began to work in publishing. Anna was taken to be a beautiful blonde chameleon whose main function was to decorate M&S and agree with everything Jack McClelland said. Given his reputation of being an awesomely dynamic explosion of publishing genius and anti-authoritarian, shit-kicking ego, it was not unreasonable to imagine that McClelland might be able to control even someone as impressively beautiful and cultured as Anna Szigethy seemed to be—it only happened not to be true.

I sat down in the chair opposite her desk and started wondering whether I should take the manuscript out of my briefcase. Despite her youth, Anna Szigethy seemed to me so polished, assured and made-up that she might have just stepped out of some fifties movie in which she was starring as a mysterious and sinister businesswoman. Unfortunately this wasn't the kind of movie in which I could have even a small part—or perhaps I was to be the clueless garage attendant accidentally run over by the sinister businesswoman's cigar-smoking accomplice.

"Nice of you to come and see me," she opened.

I rejected the idea of taking out my manuscript. Instead I started rolling a cigarette.

"I read your book." She was smiling quite broadly and I had to keep from laughing. The idea of this woman trying to make something of my fragmented psychedelic manuscript about an Ottawa Valley rock-and-roll singer was hilarious. The only thing that wasn't fun was that I was going to have to walk out of this misappropriated warehouse and back to my truck carrying her copy of my pitifully misplaced effort. All the coffee I'd drunk was now an acidic bog in my stomach.

"I really don't know what to tell you," she said.

The bog began to roil. Before another five minutes passed I was going to have to find a bathroom. Amazing how such a trivial emergency can take precedence over the fact that your life has just been ruined.

"I really think we might be able to make something out of it."

I imagined her spreading out the pages of my manuscript and dabbing them with different colours of nail polish. "Something you could publish?"

"That's what we do here," she said in a dry voice I would learn was as close as she ever came to sarcasm.

And, in fact, publishing *was* what McClelland & Stewart did. About a hundred books a year, it seemed, which reflected Jack McClelland's powerful desire to publish a list that would include every writer of interest in the country, because as well as being the saint of Canadian publishing, Jack McClelland also wanted to shape, dominate and control it.

By the time I actually met McClelland, I was utterly intimidated by his public image as a heavy-drinking chain-smoking crocodile-skinned fighter pilot turned publisher and swordsman. When I went into his office he was sitting at his desk talking on his telephone, shirtsleeves rolled up and collar open. He was sipping a glassful of clear liquid, which he kept replenishing from a thermos reputed to contain straight vodka except when he was feeling ornery, at which times it was filled with grain alcohol.

He waved me to sit down, terminated his conversation, and turned to me saying, "So, you're the new hotshot." He squashed the cigarette he was smoking into an overcrowded ashtray and started a new one.

Not to be outdone I began rolling a cigarette of my own, my shaking hands spraying tobacco all over his rug.

"Well, I haven't read it, but I hear it's great and that's all I need to know."

When I told Dennis Lee that M&S was going to publish my novel, and that I had actually seen the new executive editor to confirm this, he responded, "Oh—that must be Anna what's-her-name. The new blonde one."

"You're blond too," I replied, but seemed to find this wittier than he did.

The publication of *Johnny Crackle Sings* was a refreshing change from my previous experience. Aside from the fact that I was reviled on *This Country in the Morning* as an immoral drug-soaked hippie seeking to lead the younger generation into decadent barbarism, it was very well received by my meagre standards. Nor was the transition from being a small press author doubted by his own editor to the young whip at M&S entirely painful. Suddenly I was seen, by at least a dozen people, as the hip leading edge of Canada's most influential publishing house. This was more like it! There were divertissements, there were interviews, there was a party at Grossman's Tavern, there was a national tour that took me from Halifax to Victoria to do readings and more interviews. There were the usual Toronto literary parties at which I would encounter people from Anansi who would congratulate me on my unexpected success. There was, eventually, a small second printing as well as rumours, which came to nothing, of a Governor General's Award. There was even a coffee meeting with Robert Weaver, during which a radio drama of *JCS* was commissioned. (I wrote the script, but it was so far ahead of its time that it has yet to be produced.) True, when plotting my comeback from *Korsoniloff*, I had envisioned world fame and Hollywood. But what actually happened was enough to restore my confidence. I rededicated myself to the typewriter.

During and between drafts of *JCS* I had already started work on another novel. Perhaps I had watched *The Horse's Mouth* a few too many times on late-night television, because I decided to set the new novel in a downtown Toronto warehouse being used as a painters' studio (by coincidence I happened to know a group of painters who occupied just such a warehouse) and to structure it as a parable-parody about the idea of art as religion and the artist as half-conscious martyr. The ideas at play in the novel bore an uncanny resemblance to my interpretation of certain ideas that had been bandied about the Anansi basement office. Given the painful experience I went through with them, I was delighted to get my designated victim onto his metaphorical cross.

Needless to say the novel was riddled with problems, the most important being that except for a scene about a dying pigeon it was entirely unconvincing in every way, and so I began spending more time working on short stories.

I have always been full of ideas about what novels can or cannot be, and have always taken them seriously both as an art form and as a medium that reflects and influences social consciousness. In addition, I have always cared about my own novels being well published, well reviewed, successful, etc. Short stories, on the contrary, I have always treated as an opportunity for a vacation. There are all sorts of rules about what makes a story work, but I regard such rules as antiquated instructions, best ignored. For me, each individual story is an adventure embarked upon for its own sake. A story can take a weekend to write, or it can require numerous drafts spread out over months or even years. If I enjoy working on a story I keep working on it. If not, it finds its way into one of those numerous cardboard folders that eventually wind up at the back of my filing cabinet. Even my short story books have been fortuitous events. There isn't a big market for stories, compared to novels, but occasionally one of my publishers, out of guilt or weak-mindedness, has suggested I publish a collection. When that happens I always say that I just happen to have such a manuscript in my office, and that after doing a few last revisions I'll be glad to hand it in. Needless to say, what exists in my office (it is *my* office after all) is largely fictional. Nonetheless, a given item can usually be coaxed into existence with a few sleep-deprived weeks of frenzied typing.

When Anansi decided that a book of stories would provide a happy ending for the tortuous and awkward dealings surrounding the publication of *Korsoniloff* and *JCS*, I was eager to agree, and I did have a pile of stories I'd been writing and showing to Robert Weaver. Combined with recyclable excerpts from my failed artist's parable, they would make up enough material for a book. But it was clear that more stories had to be written.

The first step was to introduce me to my new editor, Margaret Atwood. She was an old friend and university colleague of Dennis's who had been out of the country for the start-up of Anansi. Now that Dave Godfrey had moved on to New Press, Atwood had joined Anansi's new board of directors and was actively involved in the direction of the press.

Atwood was slight and elfin, with a mop of frizzy hair, piercing eyes, a sharp tongue and a manner that was both brusque and friendly. I was already intimidated by her poetry and her success, but the fact that Dennis had confidence in her editorial capacities was most frightening of all. After a one-beer conversation during which I said I was writing more new stories for the eventual collection, we agreed to meet again when I had a more complete manuscript.

Susie and I were starting our second winter at the farm. During the year and a half we'd been there, writing had increasingly become the all-absorbing obsession of my life. Not that I was immune to the pleasure of where we were living—on the contrary. I spent hours every day roaming our land and the farms that adjoined it. Even now, almost thirty years later, I can picture every tiny corner of that farm, retrace every step of every walk that I took, remember the places where the snow lasted the longest, the trees that threw the best shade in the summer, the secret locations where I could find morels in the spring, the hills with the best wild strawberries, the meandering paths of the streams, the rust-streaked boards of the maple sugar shack, the abandoned foundations of the houses and barns built by the families who had tried to settle there, all of whose histories and tragedies I knew, thanks to the neighbours.

But none of this had anything to do with being a farmer. We had animals, a broken-down tractor with which I ploughed the garden, and I could fix my truck, wield a chainsaw or an axe or even—very reluctantly—a garden spade. Yet all this only added up to my being able to live as a city person in the country. Certainly the weak cave-chested city boy who'd moved to the country could now (if he was inspired by something like renovating his own study) work hard for hour after hour. But actually becoming a farmer or in some other way making my living through physical labour was out of the question. My attachment to what surrounded me and all its physical manifestations was total, but my relationship was that of witness, observer and worshipper.

Of course I felt somewhat guilty about this. By now we were well aware that the rural areas north of Kingston were dotted with idealistic hippies and converts to the macrobiotic organic subculture that had become the focus of the remains of the idealistic sixties generation. Theoretically I found all this attractive. I admired people who had goat farms and made their own cheese, or had gardens big enough to feed themselves year round and workshops from which they produced handcrafted furniture, quilts or weavings, all to be sold not through department stores but at various fairs.

But digging made my back tired and had I tried to make furniture I would have cut my fingers off. I didn't want to spend the winter eating root vegetables or taking care of goats birthed in my very own kitchen. I knew all this made me a traitor to my denim jacket, my pickup truck, my uncut curly hair. It also made it difficult to foresee what kind of future I could possibly have living in this place, though I loved it more than any place I had ever lived, and felt truly at home for the first time in my life.

In the meantime I had a book to finish.

The season was winter, and as one of my characters remarks in a recent story, winter has always been my season. Because I was born in December, because there's something about frozen ground and first snows that crystallizes and invigorates, because in winter the nights are long and I have always been one of those persons for whom what can't be seen at night is much more persuasive than everything that is so pressingly obvious during the day. Also, in the country, winter is the great procrastinator—all that snow and ice has the beautiful advantage of covering over and forcing the postponement of most outside work until spring.

More than ever before, writing swallowed up my life. I would work from late evening until dawn, then go out in the first light, skidding across the ice and snow to the barn, where I would give the cattle their daily ration of oats and hay while the sun rose. Back in the house I would peek into my study to see the satisfying stack of pages I had written, then return to the kitchen where I'd have break- fast and a few final cups of coffee. Sometimes these rein- forcements would wake me up so much I'd end up outside again, skiing back towards the small cedar woods with its stream or walking along the road. More often though a full belly would send me to bed where I'd pass out instantly, not to wake until late in the afternoon when the sky was beginning to turn.

I was intoxicated with the act of writing, the sound of my typewriter, the accumulating drifts of yellow news- print that curled at the bottom and often had little strands of red glue hanging from the top. I loved the compact look of words on the page, the look of typed pages on which whole sections had been scratched out, rewritten, glued or taped into place. I loved the look of a story complete, being able to say to myself, *There, that's done*, as if I had just constructed a barn or at least an outhouse, even though I hadn't constructed anything at all because soon the story would be ripped apart, cut to shreds and laid out in pieces on my desk while I stared at it despairingly at three in the morning wondering what could have led me to be so happy about this small collec- tion of yellow scrawled-over garbage.

The manic-depression of sleeplessness, I would say to myself. Bad drugs. Growing pains. But against these and other such explanations a new truth began to form. Whereas once, on my return from France, I had been blocked in the normal way—i.e., unable to write at all—I was now suffering from a special kind of writers' anti-block altogether my own: compulsive logorrhea. Write, yes, I could write. My typewriter was spitting out five, ten, even fifteen pages a night. I had swallowed the pill of automatic writing, was happy to believe that what I had to say was buried in my unconscious and required only nimble fingers and a few joints to find its way onto my desk. But alas, what was arriving was just reams of surface. Descriptions of people going from A to B. Getting dressed. Eating breakfast. Doing doing doing. But none of it mattered because the people were two-dimensional, totally without texture or gravitas, and what they were doing, whether peeling an apple or making love or dying a horrible death, was absolutely meaningless.

Looking back to see how I'd solved or avoided this problem in the past, I began to realize that it wasn't only my current writing that had this problem—so did all the work I'd published. *Korsoniloff*, with its broken syntax and semi-comprehensible plot, had only avoided the appearance of being ridiculously shallow by being, instead, incomprehensible. *JCS* had taken the process one step further, scrambling the pieces with such dexterity that the reader's eye was temporarily distracted by the juggling act.

Then I remembered that the same feeling, an inability to break through some indefinable barrier, had overtaken me when I was having so much trouble revising *JCS*. This recurring fear wasn't simply a fear, it was the uncomfortable reality of my limitations. Perhaps my desire to write had been genuine—how laudable!—but the evidence in front of me suggested that it was time to turn my non-talents to something useful.

I cannot count the number of times in my life I've told myself to quit writing and do something useful. As a prescription it sounds so good, and makes so much sense—but what does it mean? How could I, in fact, be useful?

As a social worker? When I was growing up in Ottawa my mother had been a social worker, and of course I had met some of her colleagues. Aside from those who were more or less substitute mothers, a role for which I was ill-suited, there were a couple of male street workers with an inner toughness and self-knowledge that must have made them truly valuable to their clients. However, these were exactly the qualities I lacked.

How about social work for writers—teaching creative writing? I could join the legion of writers who couldn't write and instead communicated their skills to others. I imagined myself in a leather vest (an item I would not otherwise have been caught dead in) ten or twenty years older, face trenched with cynicism. This would surely be even less of a favour to my students than my incarnation as a teacher of religion had been.

Plumbing or carpentry? I could fill the houses of innocent strangers with unexpected leaks, construct for them the same kind of awkward make-do structures that marred my own house. If I couldn't be useful, I told myself, I could at least make some money. I ghost-wrote a government report, and then decided I deserved a break before taking my next step in the working world—I went back to the typewriter.

Early in the New Year I had to go to Toronto for a couple of days. Most of my friends now had jobs, however unsatisfactory, and were more or less immersed in the daily grind of putting in long hours for low pay. Their only compensation was the fantasy of somehow breaking free of the treadmill to do something like—well, to be exact, something like what I was doing. Living in the country, getting a free ride from life, being responsible to nothing but the whims of the day.

I couldn't argue. The prospect of moving back to the city and being once again part of the dark landscape of Toronto January slush was too depressing. One night, in the house where I was staying, a woman spent several hours explaining to me that she was going to attain enlightenment by the simple method of ridding her body of all mucus, and that thousands of other subscribers to this brilliant idea had already done so. She herself had a terrible cold, which I took to be part of the exercise. She gave me a pamphlet called "The Mucusless Diet." Apparently most of our bodies are clogged with dozens of pounds of mucus, mostly as a result of the unhealthy foods we've been eating all our lives. The pamphlet rated different foods in terms of their mucus-causing properties. Meat was out, needless to say, as was anything with fat, and many grains and vegetables. The only entirely mucusless food was grapes, although after several months of cleansing, the body could take on other foods as well. Utopian note: parents who have been mucus free for several years are able to give birth to a mucus-free baby.

The next night, afraid of being left alone in the house with the mucus lady, I went to a party with some friends. This party was at the house of someone I didn't know, and was so crowded that as soon as we got in the door I lost contact with my friends and found myself wandering through a series of chemically fuelled Hieronymus Bosch-like tableaus that made me wish I was spending the evening in the barn with my cows.

The air was thick with smoke from the joints that were being passed around, and I suddenly found myself with the uncomfortable feeling that I was trapped in the midst of an insanely overcrowded subway car that was never going to stop.

Thinking a drink of water might help, I forced my way to the kitchen. There, a group of people were gathered around a woman who was talking incredibly quickly in a high-pitched voice that went straight to the bone. I was too stoned to be able to make out what she was saying, or perhaps her hypnotic effect was due to the fact that she wasn't saying anything at all, but her dentist-drill voice, her jabbing finger and her body dancing with the electricity of her own power had everyone breathless and silent. She was like some sort of circus barker, a powerful and malign female witch who had stolen everyone's soul. I couldn't resist her. Forgetting my water, I pushed through until I was in the inner circle, just a few feet away from her, mouth open, gawking. By now I could hardly hear her voice. The waves of her powerfulness were blotting out everything else and I was being battered by those waves, pushed back and forth like a piece of driftwood being worked towards the shore. I had lost all sense of direction, the strings of gravity had cut loose, I was swaying back and forth and then suddenly I was falling. Pitching forward, as they say, head first, and as I toppled, the bubble of confusion broke and I was snapped into a perfect lucidity I'd never before experienced. I'm falling, I said to myself. Indeed I was. Very slowly, but absolutely inexorably, my face was moving towards the floor. People will think I'm fainting, I thought. People will think something is wrong. But I wasn't losing consciousness, I was gaining it. Later on a friend told me that I had just keeled over, fallen like a log onto the patterned linoleum of the kitchen floor. I was scarcely aware of the impact. I just lay on the floor, grateful to have somehow escaped from the subway car, and began reassuring everyone that no, I was absolutely fine, in fact had never been better, my sincere apologies for interrupting.

The next morning I went back to the country and began writing with a confidence and freedom that were entirely new to me. Over the next few months the stories for my collection *Columbus and the Fat Lady* emerged in rapid succession as though they'd been in the wings the whole time, just waiting to be discovered. I wrote rapidly, without thinking about what I was doing, content to accept whatever came, knowing I could worry about revisions later.

One of the pieces that emerged was the first chapter of *The Disinherited*. I didn't know I was starting a new novel; I thought it was another story. But after the first few lines I knew I was on to something, a kind of naturalistic realism that had never worked for me, and quite frankly was fuelled by exactly the kind of descriptive aesthetic impulse I had always considered should be avoided in all fictional genres.

But this was different. For once the realism was *real*. I had been captured by the character who had broken onto the page—the dying farmer Richard Thomas—in a way no one I'd written about had affected me before.

Meanwhile, I had my own sentimental problems. Despite my deep attachment to the life Susie and I were living, my frenzied devotion to writing was crowding out everything else. Although I didn't know it, by the time I was finished with *The Disinherited* both my relationship with Susie and my life at the farm would be destroyed, along with whatever confidence I'd had in myself as a human being—which, fortunately, was not much.

The prospect of what was to come shadowed every word of that first chapter. When I finished it I put it aside, knowing it didn't belong with the stories and afraid to continue. Nonetheless, during those weeks I was officially ignoring it, the weave of naturalism, personal histories and disjointed time—all joined to the land and dependent on it—grew in my imagination into the long complex arc that eventually became the four Salem novels. For almost a decade I would work out that original vision; and when I finally forced myself to emerge by announcing that I'd written my last one, it wasn't because I was no longer compelled by the people I had been writing about, but because I needed a fresh start from other sources.

In the winter of 1972 the strange lucidity that had come over me the night I fainted in Toronto continued to drive my writing. My consciousness was in a state of such hysterical overexcitement that it seemed completely normal and even easy to work out the novels in one part of my mind while another part was writing *Columbus and the Fat Lady*. Each of those stories seemed to appear from a deeper place in my unconscious, emerging more like strangers I'd met in an all-night diner than contrivances that I'd deliberately put together.

Sometimes, when I had a new story or two, I'd drive my truck into Kingston where I'd get them photocopied. Usually it would be in the morning after an all-night session of writing. I'd be unshaven, clammy-handed, dazzled by the sun on the snow and trembling with too much coffee. While the stories were being copied I'd have a greasy breakfast at a nearby restaurant and address envelopes to the various targets: Robert Weaver at the CBC, Margaret Atwood and Dennis Lee for Anansi. Of course I knew they didn't really want these stories sent to them, one at a time, but I needed to be sending them, because I needed readers—even if only two or three—and because I needed to get them away from me, out of my system and into the world, before I could write the next one.

When the last story, "Columbus and the Fat Lady" itself, emerged, I knew I had totally depleted all of my resources. I was almost thirty years old. Since leaving my job at McMaster I had been writing steadily for four years. Finally I had discovered my own voice.

There are two kinds of writers: confessional writers whose main subject is themselves, and those whose main subject is others. Many of the contemporary male writers

who interested me as a teenager had belonged to the confessional camp. Norman Mailer, Ernest Hemingway,
Henry Miller all wrote fiction that was a thinly or not at
all disguised version of their own experience—complete
with those cosmetic and dramatic exaggerations that
would flatter the author as picaresque hero. In that same
line, though of course more anti-heroic than heroic, might
be put such basically solemn writers as Dostoyevsky and
Camus, or comic geniuses such as Charlie Chaplin or
Woody Allen. In all these cases we get some version of the
writer-narrator as protagonist, and all books by a given
confessional writer tend to be about the same protagonist
even if there are minor changes in name and costume.

It seemed to me that there was a spark of vitality in the
confessional writing that was lacking in novelists more
dedicated to portraying a social canvas. As a young reader
I preferred Dostoyevsky to Tolstoy, Norman Mailer to
Upton Sinclair, Albert Camus to Jean-Paul Sartre. On the
other hand the truly memorable characters of fiction often
came from the social novelists: Tolstoy's Anna Karenina,
Flaubert's Madame Bovary and Saul Bellow's Herzog all
tugged at me in a way the confessional characters of their
contemporaries did not.

Of course this division is to a certain extent arbitrary.
"Madame Bovary, c'est moi," Flaubert claimed when asked
for the sources of his famous heroine. And perhaps
Flaubert *is* every one of the dozen main characters in
his novels. But those characters—at least to the reader—
seem essentially different from each other. Even for his
masterpiece *A Sentimental Education*, which in so many
ways mirrored his own growing up, Flaubert looked not

only into the mirror but also into history books. He spent years researching the historical events surrounding his own youth, and the novel he wrote was not only a portrait of the corruption of its narrator, but a simultaneous portrait of the simultaneous corruption of a certain strain of French political idealism.

My discovery of my own voice came along with the realization that I was the kind of writer who wrote much better when I was writing about other people. Only when it was about other people did my writing seem to have the freedom, the texture, the conviction, that had been so lacking from my earlier efforts, all of which had centred on various imaginary versions of myself. By "other people" I mean not friends or neighbours or historical figures, but characters who somehow appeared full-blown in my imagination. Where they came from I don't know, and although their elements must have in many ways been drawn from my own lived or observed experience, my best characters have tended to be very different from me in age, sex and circumstance, and therefore to have lived lives quite different from my own.

Escape! the reader will say. *He just uses writing to escape his own banal reality.* How exactly true. I wanted to escape not only a minute examination of my own soul, a prospect I've always found infinitely boring, but also the life I would have lived had I not been writing, the job, the office nine-to-five, in sum the normal constrictions of being normal.

Even that winter, when my writing liberated itself, I was using writing as an escape. While I was happily hiding inside it and exulting in each new page, my so-called real life, the one I didn't want to think about, was falling apart. A few months later, my marriage to Susie undeniably in ruins, I packed a few cardboard cartons of belongings into the back of my truck and drove away from the farm. To keep my mood at a nice saw-edge I had recently quit smoking. I bumped along the road surrounded by a delightful mixture of malign thoughts, craving and contempt, fantasies of revenge and suicide—all urged on by the demons of self-destruction and self-pity that were performing their gleeful dance around me. After a few disastrous detours during which anyone around me became targets, perhaps especially those trying to help me, I ended up living in a cheap third-floor apartment in the Christie Pits area of Toronto.

All I wanted was to be alone to ride out this storm of paranoia and self-hatred (in which I took a perverse pleasure) and of course to write. Writing was all I could do, though I couldn't necessarily do that. Writing was my only friend.

The Disinherited didn't care that I was a pitiful post-sixties refugee fallen on evil times because I'd been too busy having fun and obsessing to learn anything about living. *The Disinherited* was a universe mostly inhabited by people entirely unlike me. They had their own problems, but they had chosen me to tell their story, and they were determined to stuff it in one end and shake it out the other no matter how much I snivelled and complained.

My third-floor apartment had steeply slanted eaves, which exceeded six feet only in that ridge centre where the landlord had placed the wall separating "the bedroom" from "the kitchen."

In the bedroom, which was also the living room, the sanatorium, the chamber of memory horrors, etc., the floor was mostly occupied by two items: a mattress and a small, genuine purple-patterned Persian rug I'd bought for $18.95 at Honest Ed's, which was now so generously shedding its royal fuzz that I had to brush my clothes before going out.

The kitchen had a refrigerator, but because I thought I might be in a movie I kept my beer in cases on the white Arborite table. There was also a stove, a half-sized bathroom with a half-sized bathtub, and a sink. I always had the window open because the landlord, who lived in the basement and suffered endless economies in order to pay alimony to his estranged wife and spoiled daughter, spent his off-days boiling tomatoes, which gave off a thick alkaline odour that rose through the house like a miasma from purgatory.

My routine began first thing in the morning. I would make coffee in the percolator, then retreat to my mattress to work. There I spent my mornings, drinking the coffee down to the grounds and puffing fat cigarettes of the weak dope I was using to substitute for the tobacco I had so nobly renounced.

I had yellow-lined notepads on which I would write by hand, but even this simple act caused my body to ache and a headache to install itself. I had begun *The Disinherited* full of the optimism of finding my own voice, but since my life had collapsed the act of writing—the passion for which I had apparently traded human compensations—had turned into a tortuous play in which I was a ventriloquist's dummy being jerked around by characters I myself had supposedly invented. These people were forcing me

to be them, to live every detail of lives too long, too different, too utterly beyond my experience for me to bear. Yet
who was I, a useless little shit who'd wrecked everything
around him, to refuse these people, whose voices held the
only tone of authenticity I had ever heard.

At the end of the morning I would take my yellow
sheets to the kitchen table and position them between my
typewriter and the carton of beer (in fact, I hardly drank
beer at the time, but I was convinced someone might come
to visit me). I'd make myself a couple of sandwiches, then
set off into the great outdoors.

Toronto in the early seventies had traded in its unconvincing affair with sixties glamour for a boutique-
enhanced version of fifties Hogtown. Yorkville was the
perfect example. Once a somewhat charming jumble of
run-down Victorian houses, some of them converted into
coffee houses and shops, it had by now begun a slow mer-
cenary climb to its present status of providing shopping
opportunities for tourists and those rich enough to stay at
the luxury hotels that surround it.

The area I lived in was only a couple of kilometres away
but it was untouched by such ambitions. Houses were
something people lived in not to impress each other but
to have a place to sleep and eat. Every item in every store
was always on sale, yet as I walked the grey infinity of
Bloor Street sidewalk that took me from Christie to
Spadina, I was never in danger of being tempted to buy
what I couldn't afford.

By the time I arrived at my first destination, the Jewish
Y at Spadina, I would have worked off my lunch and be

ready for some exercise. By about two o'clock I was on the running track, a short oval (eighteen laps to the mile) above the gym where I would execute my daily two-mile penance in total solitude. Now I was keeping in shape, not because I had boasted to Susie that I could do such a ridiculous thing, but because I had become convinced that writing this novel was like training for a marathon. It wasn't something that could be accomplished in a day or a week, but required an infinite well of patience and endurance.

After the run I would get a basketball from the office and begin shooting baskets. The gymnasium windows were along the west wall and if the sun was out the light would play its games across the floor while I lost myself in the intricacies of various absurd shots and feints.

Shooting baskets had always been a form of relaxation for me. My father had bolted a backboard to the garage when I entered high school and during the snow-free months I would spend an hour every day—more during exam time—learning to play and to execute essential trick shots my coaches usually failed to admire.

Now in my relative old age, basketball still plays the same role—even now I have a backboard and net nailed to a tree outside my cabin. Unlike running it has nothing to do with discipline or self-improvement. It's like stories compared to novels: a time to fool around and daydream.

One day I was taking some shots when someone else came into the gym, bouncing a basketball. He was about my height, very muscular and athletic; without even looking at me he dribbled over to the basket at the opposite end and began shooting.

Every day for about a week this same routine recurred. I would glance at him covertly, but I never caught him looking at me. From time to time his basketball or mine would roll towards the other end. It would be returned in total silence.

Finally, I cracked and asked him if he wanted to play. It was one of those days (like almost every day) when I hadn't spoken to anyone since waking up. Soon we were playing fiercely competitive games of one-on-one almost every afternoon. After a week he took the initiative and introduced himself, and after that we greeted each other and shook hands every day before we played. But beyond that we never spoke. Even during Sunday morning pick-up games we would only acknowledge each other with a nod although we'd often contrive to get on the same team and, possibly because we knew each other's game so well, were probably the only people on the floor who actually wanted to pass the ball.

Sometimes, after exhausting myself at the Y, I'd go back for another round of writing. More often, however, I was too tired to be locked up with myself again, and I'd head over to the Coach House Press to see what was happening.

It used to be said that everyone who worked at the Coach House Press was given a tab of acid every morning. This rumour, like others that portrayed Coach House as a free-living, free-loving irresponsible haven for people who decided for themselves that they were writers, then took off all their clothes and printed whatever they wanted to without getting anyone's permission, was probably meant to be apocryphal. In any case it wasn't true and it also missed the point. Drugs were far too plentiful and available to require rationing or distribution, and besides, few people came to work in the morning. What was liberating and unique about Coach House was that it was a community that had given itself over to the exploration of aesthetics and aesthetic experience, in truth more visual than verbal. Oh, the scorn that was heaped on these bedraggled hippies for caring more about art than commerce. But why? At twenty-five years old should poets be worrying about how to increase their audience to 113 people or should they be exploring the possibilities of verbal expression? Should photographers be worrying about getting a commission for a hot magazine or a real estate flyer, or should they be trying to create images that express and expand the core of their own imagination?

Although Coach House did print and sell books, in the late sixties and early seventies, it was less a commercial press than a movement. This put it in step with the new political currents of the time, but of course in opposition to the much more old-fashioned political and literary precepts of both the old-line houses like M&S and Macmillan and their would-be successors like Anansi and New Press.

Scholars may one day compare the texts published by these and other publishing houses to see if the idea of differing aesthetics has any validity. For me what was significant in those years was the kind of editorial/aesthetic discussions that seemed to typify the literary community.

At Coach House everything was questioned: the nature of narrative, the very acceptability of narrative itself, the nature and construction of sentences—I remember one particularly nasty multi-hour discussion about whether it was permissible to use adjectives, after which I stormed out of the press full of self-righteous fury, convinced that the entire history of literature was on my side.

In this instance I had been arguing that if adjectives weren't necessary as qualifiers, there would be more nouns. Victor Coleman, along with David Young (another Coach House regular), regarded adjectives as cheap make-up that could add only inauthenticity, not nuance.

Okay, you may be saying, when you're young and don't have a job, why not argue about such stupid matters? But are they really stupid? Many of the previous century's best-known and sometimes best writers of English prose had thoroughly developed theoretical ideas on what and how to write. Ernest Hemingway loved to go on about the use of Anglo-Saxon words versus Latinate words. Somerset Maugham's ideas on narrative structure were fully developed and articulated. And James Joyce or Virginia Woolf on syntax . . . To say nothing of Henry James, who late in his life decided that his own ultimate expression was best attained through the process of dictation, and therefore redictated all of his earlier works, lengthening and circumlocuting at every opportunity, then suppressed the very publications that had established his reputation, to allow the new, wordier versions to reign unchallenged.

Coach House Press had no Henry James or Virginia Woolf (though of the latter it had many a fervent follower) but it nonetheless bubbled with the energy of a twenty-four-hour-a-day debating forum where everything was always open to question, and everyone always open to new solutions and formulations.

Despite the arguments, Coach House was the place I felt most comfortable. I had even been given an official job, selecting the stories for that year's edition of the annual fiction anthology, *The Story So Far.* This meant that when I came in I could get my mail and take out my file as though I were a real employee, then go up to the kitchen table and have a cup of coffee while carefully poring over the fractured offerings.

At Anansi the editorial process as I had experienced it was centred on entirely different questions. Dennis Lee regarded prose as a kind of philosophical music. He would try to isolate the inner premises of the thought (I sometimes imagined him waving his hands over the manuscript like a diviner moving his wand over dry soil, seeking the small clear source hundreds of feet below the surface) and keep what was consistent with those premises. What rang false, either in terms of ideological substructure or linguistic discord, had to be eliminated. "Great idea!" one always imagined Dennis enthusing. "Let's just get rid of all these pages and you can start all over again and really make something of it!"

For writers like Al Purdy, Michael Ondaatje and Graeme Gibson, all writers with tremendous focus and inner consistency, Dennis was the ideal editor, because in their work there *was* a dominant mode and tone to be sensed.

For someone like me, the process had more problems. Dennis was a minister's son, I was a self-hating Jew from Ottawa. Dennis was a highly educated student of literature in the British tradition while I, in my more paranoid moments, regarded British literature as thinly disguised propaganda for imperialism, racism and anti-Semitism, to which I opposed the makeshift alternative of my own reading, rantings and hopes. Even though I'd always been interested in writing I never wanted to be an English student. Might as well convert, straighten my hair and dye it blond. Even in the anarchic atmosphere of the sixties, Anansi and the cultural nationalism it espoused had a churchy taint I found difficult to accept. Through George Grant I had come to suspect that while I could agree with the political critiques of this nationalism, the vision of the world it implied was fundamentally conservative and hierarchical in a way that made me uneasy.

At McClelland & Stewart, where I was now beginning what would be a fifteen-year association, the editorial process was even more audience-oriented. Narrative realism was taken for granted. Characters had to be physically described so that readers could visualize them and stories had to have plots that went from beginning to end. Authors were expected to write the kind of book that could find the kind of audience M&S knew how to reach.

By the time I started work on *The Disinherited* in 1972, all the technical and theoretical considerations I'd thought were the centre of the literary universe had become mere technical tools for writing the kind of books I would never have thought I could be interested in—books about people whose struggle totally compelled me, and now seemed to be not only symbolic of some great and terrible collapse, but to be that collapse itself.

In the beginning, I had tried to understand the people I met in the country intellectually. I was still under thirty, still considering the possibility of completing my Ph.D. thesis, and intellect was what I thought I had.

But once I began writing, what I "thought" seemed not to matter. For me, as it turned out, writing fiction wasn't a different version of writing an essay or a book review. It wasn't about what I "thought," it was a mysterious activity that involved being carried away by whatever voice or human reality had somehow captured me.

After Coach House, the other semi-compulsory stop on my daily rounds was a visit with TW. Sometimes we'd fill our stomachs at some inexpensive Bloor Street Hungarian restaurant, but more often we'd spend our money shooting endless games of snooker.

Tamio Wakayama's free ride at Rochdale had ended after only two years. Now he was installed in a Campus Co-op coach house, a small red-brick building in a back alley off Huron Street. Before moving in, he'd persuaded the co-op to renovate it into a living space cum darkroom and studio. To solve the financial problem, he declared war on the co-op's rent collector, a fierce capitalist witch he avoided by never answering his door, though as it turned out he did become friends with her, years later, when she'd gone into publishing (and started having children with me as a sideline).

The best time to drop in on Tamio, aside from the hours after midnight, was late afternoon. Although he often woke up while the sun was still in the sky, he didn't feel right until after 5 p.m. because, as he explained, that was the hour when most offices closed and therefore he no longer had to feel bad about being unemployed.

By the time I got there he would usually have been out to get the newspaper and would be sitting at the kitchen table drinking coffee and either examining the sports section or doing the crossword puzzle. "Hey, what's happening?" was his invariable greeting, to which I was always able to reply, "Nothing much."

When I had first met Tamio, almost ten years previously, he'd been a young hotshot photographer who'd returned to Canada with fistfuls of striking images from the U.S. civil rights movement, which he'd shot under the tutelage of a Greenwich Village photographer. Short, wiry, with straight black hair and gold-rimmed glasses, not above suddenly acquiring a Southern accent when it was useful, Tamio moved instantly to the centre of mid-sixties student politics, partly because he had actually been to the South and participated in all those events others had at best visited or watched on television, and partly because by joining politics and photography he had created himself a unique terrain (at least in Canada). He wasn't in competition with anyone else nor could he be competed with.

In the ensuing years he'd taken advantage of government initiatives such as the Company of Young Canadians, which was intended to be the Canadian domestic equivalent to the American Peace Corps, and travelled across Canada photographing everything: natives on reservations, Doukhobor villages, political demonstrations, various girlfriends in various states of undress.

He probably would have liked to be a person who took the pictures he wanted to take and somehow derived from them the money he needed to live modestly and explore the world with his camera. A nineteenth-century gentleman photographer. The only obstacles to this were, first, we lived in the twentieth and not the nineteenth century; second, he didn't come from a rich family; third, the world of art wasn't about to supply an unknown photographer with even a modest living unless said photographer made the necessary obeisances. This left him in his current situation, which was that the government money had dried up. Aside from the brief digression of Rochdale, nothing had come along to replace it except occasional freelance jobs and the fantasy of being "discovered" as a trendy art photographer whose work would then be snapped up at fabulous prices. Alas, as I learned from observing Tamio and other photographers and painters, the world of art was as cruel or crueller than the world of literature.

And in any case, why were we trying to be artists? Tamio, unlike me, had limitless confidence in the perfection of his own images, but being an artist isn't just about producing work that the producer approves of. Art is also a sociological category—other people, people who have somehow acquired the power to make such decisions, have to support the idea that a given thing is art, or that a given person is an artist.

One quality Tamio and I had in common was our complete incompetence at making our way in these matters.

December 30, 1972, was my thirtieth birthday. I was in my apartment, I was alone, I had turned the definitive corner into middle age. My face was becoming lined, the grey Toronto light could filter through my thinning hair, my best friends in Toronto were Tamio, who was keeping me alive on chicken-neck soup in return for being allowed to beat me in snooker, and the guy I played basketball with at the Jewish Y. I was about halfway through the first draft of *The Disinherited*, but I had recently shown it to a couple of people at Coach House, and they had reacted with hostility to the way I had deserted the muse of surreal experimentalism to write a novel about a farming family. It was raining globs of slush, I hadn't seen the sun for a week and hadn't been outside the city for several months. My truck was parked several blocks away, unable to start because it had a congenital problem with its distributor that I couldn't fix or get fixed. My clothes and my papers were covered in royal purple fuzz. Due to a bitter episode with his ex, the landlord had doubled the quantities of foul ingredients he put in his tomato sauce and the house smelled like a rendering plant. I was sick of smoking terrible dope instead of cigarettes so I had given that up as well, leaving me in the kind of mood that made me want to sit around shredding newspapers and grinding my teeth. A few days before a well-meaning friend had introduced me to an eligible young lady who had offered to break the spell of my loneliness but then called me "Daddy" at what might have been an intimate moment. I'd had my big January Epiphany just eleven months ago but now I felt like one of those globs of slush lying on the road and getting run over again and again by cars that had traded in their mufflers for loud sound systems.

Perhaps because my birthday falls so close to the end of the year, I've always liked to make New Year's resolutions. This time I resolved that by the time the slush stopped falling I would have finished *The Disinherited*, and further, that when it was done I would pack my apartment into my truck and drive it to the West Coast. That I would turn into someone else and never come back.

Armed with my resolution, I was no longer simply a lost soul wandering the purgatory of winter in Toronto. I was a man with a mission, a lost soul with a purpose and therefore no longer lost. To begin with, I turned into a person who was going to finish his novel so he could leave his apartment, pack his truck and drive, etc. I read through my stack of pages, restructured them and numbered them carefully. What I had was already longer than my two previous novels but still nowhere near being finished. I felt stranded in the midst of a gigantic uncrossable sea. I took my beer carton off the kitchen table and set the finished chapters out in little piles. I had six piles, but very little idea of what would happen next. Having stuck to my resolution for almost two weeks, I had an attack of doubt. Why not forget this whole project? Why not go back to writing zany short stories and finishing my thesis? Tempted to renounce the whole project I made some copies and delivered what I'd done to Dennis Lee and Anna Porter.

Meanwhile, I read and reread the sixth chapter, wondering how I could carry the story forward. That was when it came to me—as it has so many times when I'm writing, and yet it arrives every time as if I'd never thought of it before—that instead of going forwards I could go backwards.

By the time Anna and Dennis responded, both of them with an enthusiasm so generous I couldn't believe they had been reading the same scratched-up mess I'd sent them, the emotional centre of gravity of my novel had shifted. Until now it had been the struggle between the character I'd begun with, the farmer, Richard Thomas, and his sons Erik and Brian. Now a surface of complications had peeled away and what was revealed was Richard's father, Simon, a tough unyielding crank who'd walked and ruled his land with a joyful tyranny that had terrified and scarred all those around him.

It was July before the first draft of the whole novel was done. Exhausted, I gave notice to my landlord, packed my truck and headed for the West Coast. Over the months that followed I made some minor cosmetic changes, but the process of writing even the imperfect manuscript I had produced had been so painful I couldn't face revisiting it. In fact, I have never reread it, and when the time came to check the proofs, I had to ask a friend to do it for me.

CanLit

Years

----

search to figure out what being
a writer is, post DTs... move from
national to international

ith the publication of *The Disinherited* in 1974, I was in the very fortunate position of having written the right book at the right time. Although it appeared briefly on some best-seller lists it wasn't really a commercial hit. Nor was it read outside the country, except by agents and by publishers who turned it down. But within Canada, it did well and secured me my own small blotch on the literary landscape.

As the seventies wore on—and to a child of the sixties, wearing on was what the seventies seemed to be doing—the strong winds of Canadian nationalism first grew to hurricane force, then began to drop.

Not that Canadian writing failed to prosper. Many of those writers now considered to be our greatest—Robertson Davies, Timothy Findley, Margaret Laurence, Margaret Atwood, Alice Munro—gained unprecedented audiences, sales, international recognition, and most of all a dominant place in the Canadian public imagination. All of them were writing out of a conservative, small-town, restrained, Protestant tradition that found a tremendous echo of self-recognition across the country. These writers were, in effect, writing the secret diaries of their readers, finding words and images for their experiences.

But for writers of a slightly younger generation, for example the offbeat, very unconservative, unProtestant, unrestrained offspring of a completely different cultural and religious tradition, which I happened to be, no such echo was to be found. The readers, critics and teachers who would have provided it simply didn't exist—at least, not in very large numbers. Without initially realizing it, I had joined that enormous and timeless legion of writers, many more talented than myself, whose books, no matter how good, cannot easily prosper within the realm of commercial publishing.

After such a promising start with *The Disinherited* I became convinced that I was simply spinning my wheels, working harder and harder to write more and more books for fewer and fewer people.

Why bother? I began to ask myself.

On the cosmic scale of things there was no answer to this question. In fact, one less writer on a planet with too many writers producing too many books out of too few trees for too few readers would not have constituted a great tragedy.

Unfortunately, I was not in a position to embrace the cosmic view.

So far as my own options were concerned, nothing had changed since the day I drove to McClelland & Stewart hoping to persuade Anna Porter to publish my novel. Being a writer was my only option. I had no alternative. Even those I might have had no longer existed because I was older, and could no longer consider going back to graduate school or teaching at McMaster. On the other hand, because of the critical success of *The Disinherited*, and to a lesser extent the novels that followed, my options as a writer (and being a writer who was somewhat unread was no handicap) had expanded. I could write nasty book reviews to make sure no one else's books got read either; I could teach other people to become writers so they could end up as miserable as I was; I could even use my writing skills for pseudonymous activities that brought in a certain amount of cash.

Maybe my situation had improved after all.

In less than a decade, I had gone from being the desperate and confused would-be writer driving his truck to Toronto hoping for a contract for a hundred-page novella, to being, still in my thirties, a prolific "author" with several novels to my credit, of which at least one was fast becoming a staple of the newly invented realm of "Can-Lit." Why wasn't I happy?

At the time, I ascribed my unhappiness to my difficulties in the world of writing and publishing.

But, to cite a line attributed to Socrates that has always seemed to me completely absurd, as well as the height of wisdom: "All knowledge is self-knowledge." And, perhaps, it should have as its Freudian corollary: "All misery is self-inflicted."

I didn't realize it at the time, but what I had done by writing my way into the Canadian literary establishment, was to stick myself into a version of that very cage I'd spent my whole life avoiding. Of course I didn't do it on purpose: when I started writing there was no such thing as a group of established writers. There were, instead, a few individuals who by their wit, talent and luck had somehow made lives for themselves as writers.

The challenge faced by a young writer in Canada today is exactly that, but with the difference that now it's in a hot-house context of cliques, mutual support groups, creative writing schools, eager publishers and agents that could not even have been imagined thirty years ago. What existed instead, in the seventies and early eighties, was a weird bee-swarm or cloud—some considered it a self-referential miasma—of "Canadian literature," which was sustained by a combination of enthusiastic readership, government funds, dozens of courses teaching Canadian material and a loud media orchestra with an infrastructure that generated many more reviews, interviews, public appearances, etc., than the slimmed-down media world of today could or could want to provide. This Canadian literature thing was not only a Toronto phenomenon; it included writers and publishers across a country that still mostly pretended to want to think it *was* a country (though this didn't prevent the various factions from fighting each other, feeling superior to each other, blaming the ever-shrinking market for each book on each other's overly prolific existence). And in return for all this attention the writers provided the words.

The good thing was that this weird behemoth, which was always trying to bite various parts of its own body, could actually (more or less) sustain itself. The bad thing was that "diversity," as it is called today, was not a strong feature. The tunes of CanLit were too often played to very confined groups of people, and many were beginning to see it as a closed shop, totally unbalanced in terms of gender, race, ethnicity, geography and culture.

How did I fit into all this? Badly.

As the seventies drew to a close, I began to realize that the very force that was sustaining me—Canadian cultural nationalism—was also the trap from which I would have to escape.

The motherhood idea of Canadian nationalism was that Canadians should have the chance to tell themselves, in books, movies and music, their own stories. This is an idea to which I am still committed. But which Canadians get to tell what stories? Right from the first days of my editorial clashes with Dennis Lee I realized that what was called "Canadian cultural nationalism" was often an attractive Trojan horse, carrying within it exactly those conservative Christian ideals and nostalgias that I had rebelled against politically a decade ago as a student, then fled intellectually when I left George Grant and McMaster's Department of Religion.

Meanwhile, the focus of my own writing was beginning to blur. Following *The Disinherited*, I wrote three more rural novels—*Wooden Hunters*, *The Colours of War* and *The Sweet Second Summer of Kitty Malone*—in quick succession.

Of the three, only *Kitty Malone* really satisfied me, and after completing that novel I felt it was time for me to move on to something else, though what that might be, I didn't know.

In the spring of 1979, just after *Kitty Malone* was published, I went to the offices of McClelland & Stewart on a fundraising mission. It was a propitious moment: the novel had received terrific reviews and even managed to climb to the bottom of the best-seller list. And I, as usual, was flat broke.

Until now, all such visits had been to see Anna Porter. From our very first meeting about *Johnny Crackle Sings* she had been the person I worked with at M&S. Although one might think dealing with a large publishing house would be more difficult than dealing with a small one, the opposite was the case. At both Coach House and Anansi, the atmosphere was intensely competitive, and the most dismaying aspect of it all was that the writers seemed to have to compete for the approval of the editors. Of course, every writer wants to be told that each draft of each work is a production of unparalleled genius—and perhaps there are times when such a demand is unreasonable. But to feel that with each draft you risk the *contempt* of your publisher (to say nothing of the rejection of your manuscript), to get a letter from your own publisher saying he'd better not give a Canada Council reference because the reference might not be flattering—that also seems unreasonable.

In comparison, the atmosphere at the large presses I dealt with in the seventies (McClelland & Stewart and Doubleday), was quite low-key, perhaps because their editors did not regard themselves as burdened with the responsibility of shaping the future of world literature and human consciousness.

In this regard, Anna Porter had been the ideal publisher from the very beginning. For every one of my projects she had expressed enthusiasm and support. Each manuscript as it came in was, indeed, a work of genius, and the publication of each book was marked by a generous and drunken party at her house. And after publication day? Well, perhaps things went downhill, but meanwhile there was another book in the works, another protean hope just waiting to get between covers.

But by the time of this visit to M&S in 1979, Anna had left the company to run its sister company, the mass-market paperback publisher Seal Books.

The good part of this for me was that there would be an assured paperback sale for my novels. The difficult part was that I would now have to deal with Jack McClelland himself, who (I'd always been given to believe) regarded me with some scepticism, as "Anna's author."

When I went into Jack's office he was in one of his archetypal post-lunch poses: his suit jacket was off, his sleeves rolled up and his tie undone; leaning back in his chair with his feet on his desk, he was dictating into a microphone. He waved to me as I entered and continued with his blistering tirade (in perfect sentences and paragraphs) while taking the odd sip from the glass on his desk, which he kept filled from a thermos widely assumed to hold vodka.

When he finished he apologized for keeping me waiting, put the dictaphone away and turned to face me. As he did so he took out a large pad and a pen. My paranoia was such that I thought he was planning to sketch out his next letter while I was talking. I would learn, in fact, that he always took notes during conversations, often pages worth. I suspect he later just crumpled them up and threw them in the wastebasket, but there was something very psychologically effective about this tactic. Somehow it turned the tables without really changing anything.

"What can I do for you?"

I stammered out that I wanted to discuss my next project.

McClelland looked at me blankly.

Here it comes, I thought, now that Anna's gone he can just get rid of me.

"Your next project," he said. "Do you have one?" Every article written about Jack McClelland emphasized his blazingly intense blue fighter-pilot eyes. They were trained on me now, but as he reached for his glass I wondered if his eyes were blazing with hostility or simply the desire to be having a proper drink, preferably out of the office and in the kind of situation he was said to find much more congenial.

"Not really," I admitted. "I could write another novel."

"Yes," McClelland said in his sardonic way. "You *could* write another novel. Would you like some money for it?"

"Yes," I said. How had this happened? Not a flicker of a smile crossed McClelland's face.

"How much?"

I shrugged. "As much as I can have, I guess."

McClelland nodded. "What's it going to be about?"

I described a science fiction novel set in San Francisco, whose hero, a cult leader, believed he had mysterious knowledge and mystical powers due to the fact he'd once been a dolphin. I said I wasn't too sure about it.

McClelland nodded in agreement. "What about something else along the line you've been doing? Could you go back to the well one more time?"

There was something tired in his voice. He had done his duty, and now he was asking me if I could do mine. I had the germ of an idea for another rural novel—it eventually became *Flowers of Darkness*, the last of the Salem novels—and as I talked about it I knew that his phrase "back to the well one more time" perfectly described my situation. I wasn't tired of writing fiction and I hadn't lost interest in writing about the country, but somehow the prospect of knowingly repeating myself had all the attraction of setting out to dig a ten-mile ditch.

On the other hand, I knew that repeating myself—not too much and not too blatantly—might well be what readers wanted. Writers have their niches, their ways of writing. People want to know what to expect when they pick up your book. The problem was that having fled in horror from a civil service town, the last thing I wanted to do was to become my own civil service, mindlessly erecting a literary monument to some idea I'd had ten years ago.

In the end I took the contract and the advance, and wrote the book knowing it would be the end of a certain period for me. In terms of structure and plot it was both the most conventional and the most accomplished of the Salem novels, though its apparently commercial veneer didn't affect its sales. Meanwhile I began looking around for ideas about what the next chapter of my own writing life might be.

One of the many absurd means of making money I investigated was the writing of children's books. I hadn't had children and I knew very little about them except how to tell my friends' children silly stories. Nonetheless, in the late seventies M&S was beginning to publish illustrated children's books by well-known writers, and I was quick to take advantage of what seemed to me easy money. This resulted in a book called *The Leaves of Louise*, whose principal distinction was that it was voted the scariest children's book of the year by a group of Ottawa schoolchildren. I was tremendously flattered until I found out the reason it had won was the strange purple of the illustrations. I also ended up writing a couple of children's stories for magazines.

This dazzling corpus made me, in my own mind, quite an expert, and certainly the possessor of a wallet ready to be filled. When in the fall of 1978 I was invited by a friend to a dinner party that would include the children's publisher Patricia Aldana, I heard the sound of opportunity knocking.

Strangely enough, as often happens with writers before meetings with publishers, by the time the dinner came I'd had a brilliant idea. Forget children's books. Even better would be dog books. Books by dogs for dogs. If children were the unexploited market of the present, dogs were surely the cash cow, so to speak, of the future.

Fortunately, I happened to have a brilliant dog who was just aching to express himself to the millions of other bookless dogs scattered across the planet. His idea was that with a camera tied around his neck he would go into a number of choice locales—swamps, skunk dens, foetid barns, butcher shops, etc.—and take photos of what he found. These photos would be reproduced as (and here was the *stroke of genius*) scratch-and-sniff illustrations. When the gift-receiving dog or its owner scratched the photo, the smell would be released. The dog would go crazy with delight! Soon the book would be torn to tatters!

What a perfect Christmas present for man's favourite animal: first adored, then destroyed.

Being the diffident sort I didn't simply blurt my idea out during dinner. I waited until afterwards. When the publisher volunteered to help with the dishes, I accompanied her into the kitchen. Then and there, wiping the odd pot, I casually described my million-seller.

Needless to say she was fascinated. She even set up a meeting to further discuss the idea. The fact that between the dinner and the time of our next meeting I tried to sell the same idea to Doubleday showed only that this was not simply a dubious proposition I was trying to pass off on a beginning publisher but an idea in which I had genuine faith.

In the end, Doubleday's New York brass "reluctantly" turned down my brain wave. Ms. Aldana never exactly said no, but as our conversations turned to other projects I began to think she might not find me a writer suitable for either dogs or children.

Fortunately, I was also being distracted by other possibilities, including that of journalism. I wasn't very good at research, but the absence of facts made my articles easier to read. When I was asked by *Quill & Quire* and *Books in Canada* to do some interviews and profiles of the older generation of writers, I leapt at the chance. Not only because I needed the work, but because arriving at my own dead end had made me interested in the question of how other writers conducted their lives.

Before I interviewed Hugh Garner I had met him perhaps a dozen times, but only for handshakes at various literary events.

Even before those encounters he was a large figure to me: first, because I had been impressed by his novel, *Cabbagetown* (1950), a skilfully plotted book about Toronto's Cabbagetown during the Depression with a tone as uncompromising as the seamy area of Toronto he was depicting; second, for his more recent short stories and journalism. His *Hugh Garner's Best Stories* had won the Governor General's Award for 1963, and he was a very prominent public figure. When I was growing up he was famous as one of Canada's most prolific and best-paid writers of magazine features, and equally legendary for his hard-living, hard-boozing ways, which had perhaps contributed to the gravelly, down-to-earth or possibly even underground quality of his voice (often to be heard on CBC-Radio).

He was also an outspoken sceptic about the fledgling Writers' Union. I didn't hold this against him—a little intergenerational scepticism is not always a bad thing— but was aware that Garner had come to be considered an old-fashioned relic of that musty and antique past that we younger writers had supposedly thrown definitively into the shadows.

We'd first met at the bizarre mass love-ins of CanLit, called "Canada Days." These occasions are almost extinct now but they were veritable skyscrapers in the literary landscape of the seventies. Over a day or two or sometimes even three, at various locations (mostly in Ontario) dozens of writers, teachers, critics and booksellers would be flown in from all over the country to some educational institution, and there, hour after hour, writers would give seminars on their work to packed houses. Some of the listeners were often quite expert and all were intent on spreading the CanLit gospel.

As the fervour for Canadian literature swept the country in the seventies, Garner's *Cabbagetown* had been reread and recognized for the classic it was. He became a popular featured guest at these literary pep rallies. A stocky lived-in ruin of a man with an unpretentious if not modest manner, Garner was of medium height, with black thinning hair combed straight back, steel-rimmed glasses and a handshake designed to weed out the sissies. In my denim jacket and workboots, always looking across the room to make sure I knew where the door was, I probably didn't make a very good impression. Nonetheless, on the occasion of the publication of his mystery novel, *The Sin Sniper*, when I called and asked for an interview, he very politely agreed and suggested I come to his apartment one afternoon for coffee. Such is the power of the press, even *Quill and Quire*.

What Garner could not possibly have known was that even though I was one of those young writers he regarded with deep suspicion, I had been developing a grudging admiration for him. I hadn't written *Cabbagetown* but I *had* written *The Disinherited*. I hadn't been one of Canada's best journalists and become known for drinking it all away, but I had experienced a downhill slide into the depths of my own contradictions.

What next? I kept asking myself. It seemed to me that Hugh Garner had, with his successful mystery novels, found himself an interesting answer to this very question. He had revived his own career, and simultaneously escaped from the literary politics of the seventies—a wise strategy, because the new wave of 1970s Canadian criticism was to abandon looking at fiction for what it was, in favour of using "texts" to confirm various European theories of deconstruction and semiotics. He had done this by moving out of the field of so-called official literature into a genre, mystery novels.

Now, twenty-five years later, this strategy is commonplace. All sorts of writers who are "taken seriously" ply their trade within what used to be such completely airtight categories as science fiction, mystery, thrillers, even romance. Decades ago, people laughed at Harold Robbins when he said he should win the Nobel Prize, but *The Bridges of Madison County* was received as though it had come from the pen of a modern Shakespeare. In fact, even Shakespeare is now culturally positioned as a writer of romantic comedy.

Garner lived in a modest apartment building in midtown Toronto. He looked a bit older and more tired than the last time I'd seen him (striding purposefully down a hotel corridor holding a large bottle of rye) and he was wearing a plaid cotton shirt, charcoal slacks and worn leather shoes that looked as though they had been polished every week for a decade.

After a well-publicized collapse and cure, Garner had become a complete teetotaller. We sat in his kitchen and drank tea while I asked him about his writing. He made absolutely no claims for his novels, saying simply that he wrote them for his own enjoyment and because he needed to make money. He probably thought that I was a literary snob, and I certainly wasn't about to confess that at that moment I so hated everything I had

written that I'd decided to give up fiction in favour of
ghost-writing, along with a parallel career of writing,
under a pseudonym, a series of science-fiction novels
about a dolphin who becomes a San Francisco guru. I
couldn't help noticing that there was something earnest
and realistic about Garner's project, and his attitude
towards it, compared to mine about my dolphin-guru
fantasy.

After about half an hour he excused himself to bring
me something, which turned out to be a set of binders
containing, carefully holed to fit into the three-ring format, all of the contracts he had received for the rights,
national and international, to publish his books.

I was meant to be impressed and I was, and not just
with the extent and success of his publishing ventures.
What struck me more forcefully was the incredible organization and focus this collection implied. What a contrast
it must have made, not only to the less directed efforts of
other writers, but to his own previous, prodigal self. After
I left, and during the time I was writing up the interview,
there was one image I couldn't shake: Hugh Garner, his
mouth spread in a smile that was not exactly genuine but
had elements both of triumph and forced politeness,
pushing his contract binders across the table for me to
inspect.

I didn't know if I was seeing a man who had defied ad-
versity or who had been forced to submit, and the puzzle
has stayed with me ever since.

When *Books in Canada* asked me to interview Morley
Callaghan, my first reaction was, to tell the truth, dismay.

When I was in high school and first becoming aware of Canadian literature, Morley Callaghan was one of the first Canadian writers that I knew about. Not only were his short stories sometimes taught, they were omnipresent in the magazines of the day, and he himself was a prominent figure on Canadian radio and television, often appearing on such popular programs as *Front Page Challenge*. Unfortunately, from the point of view of a prospective interview, Callaghan was also one of those Canadian writers who represented everything in Canadian literature that I wanted to avoid.

I had always been completely mystified by the writing of Morley Callaghan. He had a reputation as a literary innovator and modernist, but his early books seemed lifeless compared to those of his famous Paris contemporaries, Hemingway and Fitzgerald, and his later fiction appeared awkward and self-serving. The fact Callaghan was so admired by the ruling literary powers and punjabs only confirmed to me that the Canadian literary scene was a self-perpetuating tea party.

During the 1920s and part of the thirties (his own twenties and thirties) he was enormously successful, and had every reason to feel that he was to be classed with Fitzgerald and Hemingway, who have endured as world figures, their lives public parables of greatness and failure. Callaghan long survived them, but had retreated to near-invisibility on the world literary scene even as he became a veritable beacon of Canadian letters.

I agreed to do the Callaghan interview because I needed the money, and because I was curious about the man, but really it was his career that now caught my attention. Like so many Canadian writers he had started out strong only to be driven back. Was there some kind of mysterious curse that hung over our writers, or was there in each case an individual explanation?

Although my mind was made up about his books I decided to reread some of them anyway, partly to see if they were as I remembered them, but mostly, I admit, because it would have been embarrassing to interview the dean of Canadian letters without some knowledge of his work.

I was spending time in Toronto after a long stint in the country, and I had brought with me my large and energetic dog. I got in the habit of taking him for early morning walks at Christie Pits, the big bowl-shaped Toronto park that among other things is famous for an anti-Semitic riot in the 1930s; also, for more than fifty years, it has been a place where some pretty good baseball is played.

One fine summer morning, walking my dog through the park, I looked around and noticed a scattering of old men sitting on the benches, smoking cigarettes, reading newspapers, taking in a Toronto moment that has existed on summer mornings for generations. Surrounded by elderly, impoverished immigrants who had probably spent their working lives within a couple of miles of this place, I suddenly felt as though I were in a Morley Callaghan novel.

I looked again at the old men. Most of them were wearing suit jackets, sometimes even matching trousers, ties, shirts buttoned at the neck, shoes that had once been good enough to go to church and now still bore signs of encounters with black polish. These men weren't just there to be part of the decor. Unlike me (I was just passing through), these men were former *dudes*, perhaps continuing dudes;

they were part of a scene. Later in the day I would see the same men, their outfits sometimes renewed, gathered in clusters outside certain stores, eating at certain restaurants. They *knew* each other. They always had. Their lives were part of a plan and Morley Callaghan had, for a long time, tried to understand lives like these, lives of Toronto men with modest jobs who still had a thing about the way they looked, their prowess with women, the way they were seen by other men. Early in his first novel, *Strange Fugitive*, Callaghan describes Harry Trotter emerging from his job at the lumber yard "altogether aloof from the yard, no bum, not just a hunky boss, no cheap skate from a lumber yard. He walked confidently along the platform, the flash of thick blond hair under the hat brim well cut, his tanned high-cheekboned face free from stubble, his stylish tweed suit with a high waist-line, well cut and form-fitting."

If Canada were like the United States, England or France, books like *Strange Fugitive* and *The Watch That Ends the Night* would have been made into great movies, classics of self-mythologizing that would have clarified, even transformed, our view of ourselves. Instead of being simply books, they would have become part of our collective identity. But Canada does not often elevate its own cultural products to mythological status. Nor has it learned to feed on its own mythology; it prefers to import the mythology of others. *Strange Fugitive*, like virtually every other novel published before 1970, is now a museum piece instead of a living text; occasionally studied or reread as a historical artefact, it has never become an essential strand of a living cultural fabric.

By the time I actually went to see Callaghan, I had worked myself into the position of being one of his most enthusiastic defenders. One afternoon shortly after lunch, I presented myself at his Roxborough Avenue home and nervously knocked at the door.

There was a long wait—although I was exactly on time, I began to wonder if I'd made a mistake or if Callaghan had changed his mind.

Then finally the door swung open. Although he was by then well into his seventies, Callaghan appeared anything but frail: a short pot-bellied man, he exuded a certain physical force from his very centre, like a pugilistic Buddha. I introduced myself. He cocked his head and looked at me sadly, as though regretting this was the best Canada's supposedly national literary magazine could offer, then motioned me to follow.

I immediately passed on greetings from Robert Weaver, whose name, I had hoped, might ingratiate me.

"So you know Weaver?" Callaghan said.

I nodded.

"He's buying a lot of stories these days," Callaghan said grumpily, making it clear that if Weaver had bought any of mine it was to promote democracy, not literature.

His living room was large but not ostentatiously furnished. There were a lot of paintings on the walls, most strikingly a huge Kurelek of transcendent cabbages glowing in a field. The round cabbages somehow reminded me of Callaghan's tummy; I looked over to check on this while I was taking my list of questions out of my briefcase. Callaghan was waiting patiently, like a child who must go through a certain ordeal, and I found myself liking him. If only I'd had some better insight into his books. Despite my moment of sympathy in the park, the lives of his characters, their censorious attitudes and their overwhelming combination of self-repression and pride were so unfamiliar to me that his novels might as well have been science fiction.

I began by telling him how much I'd liked his new book, and thanking him for taking the time to see me.

"My pleasure," Callaghan said.

I looked down at my notes. How could I have ever thought this skimpy list of questions would get me through an hour?

"It must be a challenge," I said, "having had such a brilliant success so young, to keep writing to that same standard."

"I like to think I'm getting better," Callaghan said. "I think this is my best so far. What do you think?"

"I don't know," I said. "I really liked *Strange Fugitive*. And also *That Summer in Paris*."

"Oh that," Callaghan said. "Everyone thought it was a big deal that I was a better fighter than Hemingway. I always knew I was and so did he."

"It was a good book. Very beautifully written."

Callaghan shifted and rolled his shoulders slightly, like a boxer seeking the hands of his trainer. Perhaps that *was* the feeling he had, because he then suddenly asked me, "Do you box?"

"I'm too old," I said. "Anyway, I never did. I couldn't have taken my glasses off—I wouldn't have been able to see." I spoke in the tones of one who deeply regretted not having been able to get my face reshaped by the manly art.

"Never too old," Callaghan said. He stood up, went into a bit of a crouch, feinted a left jab. "Come on."

I imagined us stumbling around the living room, shadow boxing to some slow broken record I was unable to hear. "That Afternoon on Roxborough," I would call my article. While running away from Morley Callaghan I would bump into the Kurelek painting and get knocked out by a falling cabbage.

"I wanted to ask you about—"

The telephone rang. "Excuse me," Callaghan said.

As he left the room I realized I had indeed been saved by the bell. I had been about to ask him how he had reacted to finding himself back in the world of Canadian letters after his fling with international success. He would have hated the question—it would have implied he was a failure. How could I have even considered saying such a thing to him?

I could hear his voice. He had finished listening to whoever had called and was now offering literary advice. Write every day. Don't be afraid to meet important people. Feel free to use my name.

I looked over my list of questions and realized they were all either insulting or inane. I decided to ask him how he had become such a good boxer and whether he saw any similarities between boxing and writing. I wrote this down and then tried to think of another question. Why have you lived in Toronto all these years? That would be a good one. I'd often heard him talking about Toronto on the radio. On the other hand, perhaps he might take such a question as a criticism. Where else, after all, was he supposed to live? Was I saying there was something wrong with living in Toronto?

I flipped through my notes again, reminded myself that what I had liked about my favourite, *That Summer in Paris,* was not so much his portraits of other writers—despite my long-standing fascination with Hemingway's trousers and his theories about writing. The language was what attracted me. In this memoir Callaghan had found a style that demanded less of the reader, at least this reader. With his fiction, my problem was not the intellectual demands that it made—all of Callaghan's books provided an easy-to-read surface—but the self-assured moral superiority that surrounded the narrative voice. The Paris memoir also had traces of that moral superiority. At times Callaghan seemed to be looking down on Hemingway from such a distance the reader wanted to offer him a pair of binoculars, but perhaps because it was more obvious, I found it less objectionable.

In any case, I had written down this sentence from the book: "For the sake of their own souls most men live by pretending to believe in something they secretly know isn't true." In context, Callaghan had been referring to Ernest Hemingway's exaggerated estimate of his own boxing prowess. But I had copied out these words because I had thought it might be amusing to ask Callaghan if, in the era of wisdom after a long life, there was something he realized he had pretended to believe in. This idea had seemed inordinately clever to me when I was doing my research, but now it just further derailed me.

The truth is, I was completely unprepared for and unsuited to this interview. I should never have come. I wondered if I could slip out the door while Callaghan was still on the phone. As I was considering this retreat, he came back and sat down on the sofa. "That was my son, Barry." he said. "Do you know him?"

"We've met," I said.

"He's in Ireland," Morley Callaghan said.

There was a pause, after which we talked about the beauties of Ireland and Irish literature. Then there was another pause. He had mentioned his admiration for James Joyce in *That Summer in Paris*. While I thought about this and tried to turn it into a question about fictional modernism, the new pause became a silence. Lost, I stared at the Kurelek cabbages, desperately waiting for my mouth to open and speak. Callaghan stared down at the carpet. Finally, he coughed and stood up.

"Thank you for your time," I said as we shook hands at the door.

"My pleasure," Morley Callaghan replied.

As I walked down the steps I could feel his eyes on my back. Then the door closed behind me with a sigh that must have been our mutual relief.

It is difficult today to recreate the extent to which, in the 1970s, Margaret Laurence was *the* massive and dominating presence on the Canadian literary scene. Others, like Atwood, Davies, Richler, Moore, Munro, MacLennan, Mitchell and Callaghan, had large and loyal followings, but Margaret Laurence was the *primus inter pares*, the Queen Bee, the mother, grandmother and all the aunts of the "tribe" (a word she used and one that stuck) of Canadian writers.

Of all those writers who had been born in Canada or lived here, she was considered the best, the most Canadian, the most universal, the most gifted and the most accomplished. And of all of her many books, which were considered to be indubitable classic masterpieces, the most masterful masterpiece of all was considered to be *The Stone Angel*.

When I first happened across the novel in 1970 (it had been published to great acclaim in 1964 but I hadn't been listening), Laurence's fame, to me, was based only on her having written a book (*A Jest of God*) that got made into a movie starring Paul Newman and Joanne Woodward.

Before reading *The Stone Angel*, my exposure to "official" Canadian literature had mostly been through the poetry of Irving Layton, Al Purdy and Leonard Cohen, which I'd liked a lot, the stories of Stephen Leacock, which made me laugh, and the novels of MacLennan and Callaghan, which had seemed, by contrast, stodgily written diatribes against life.

The Stone Angel was something else. I was immediately captured and impressed by its spare and elegant prose, its unflinching stare into the soul of another human being, its total structural focus. This is *Canadian!* I kept muttering to myself. I was so impressed that I read *Fifth Business* that same weekend. And like *The Stone Angel* it bowled me over. Although in many ways it was exactly the opposite of Laurence's book in style, politics and concerns, *Fifth Business*'s complex density, the uncanny way it unfolded, its ability to juxtapose, no, its absolute *insistence* on juxtaposing, so many worlds in one book, had me again enthusing about Canadian literature, and very disloyally thinking I was unlikely to find this kind of manuscript hanging around the kitchen tables of Anansi or the Coach House Press.

I had met Margaret Laurence at a Writers' Union gathering in the early seventies, when the union was still in its earliest stages. Laurence was then in her fifties, a short, vigorous, black-haired woman with large eyes that alternated between burning straight at you and looking somewhat lost behind her old-maidish spectacles. She was about to move permanently back to Canada after long spells in Africa, then London, and there was a feeling she was coming home to take up a certain position.

In those early days of the Writers' Union—to begin with we were barely a dozen—issues of professionalism and constant discussion about writing itself had no trouble co-existing. Annual meetings would be followed by long sessions of Scotch-drinking, and on one of those occasions, in the bar of the Lord Elgin Hotel in Ottawa, I found myself sitting in a large armchair opposite Margaret Laurence. I'd exchanged various civilities with her but we'd never had a real conversation. By this point in the evening her eyes were swimming behind her glasses like large melting ice cubes; as she opened her mouth to speak I felt faintly worried that she was going to be sick.

"Matt," she said, "you of all people *must* surely understand what it takes to write fiction about real people."

I nodded sagely. Real people? What it had mainly required so far was that I smoke a lot of dope plus be willing to go completely insane by climbing out of my own mind and into someone else's. I assumed that Margaret Laurence wasn't the type to indulge in either of these activities. But as she sat there staring into my eyes and awaiting a response, it began to dawn on me that even if she was twenty years older than myself, more interested in liquor than drugs, and impossibly removed from me in dozens of other ways, this weird mind-abandoning process involved in writing about other people might be exactly what she *did* mean.

"It's not easy," I said.

"Hell it's not easy," she agreed, at which moment, to my relief, a crowd of her admirers arrived.

Graeme Gibson had more or less founded the Writers' Union and supplied a lot of the political vision that would take it through its first few years. I felt both privileged and lucky to be included when the early meetings took place; they were held on Brunswick Avenue, either at Marian Engel's house or just up the street at Austin Clarke's. Despite the fact they were only separated by a few dozen paces, the two meeting places were totally unlike.

Austin Clarke's study was the ultimate male bastion and fantasy. It was large enough to seat a dozen people (some on the floor), and lined with beautiful shelves containing a whole library's worth of books, including various editions of his own already considerable publications. Of his, I especially admired *When He Was Free and Young and He Used to Wear Silks*, which Anansi had published. Austin would sit in solitary and contented splendour behind a huge desk, his study in every way a suitable haven for "the writer."

Marian Engel's large and pleasant living room fell into the harried housewife category. It was so emphatically disorganized that it in fact overflowed the category to become its own archetype. Its furnishings were the inevitable result—though unfortunately at the time I couldn't know it—of co-existence with vigorous young children. Her ground floor workroom was behind glass doors in what had been the dining room. It looked to me like the site of a hurricane disaster, but somehow it yielded the unending stream of amazingly elegant reviews and fictions that I had thought, before meeting her, must issue from some museum of perfect orderliness.

Margaret Laurence, on the other hand, seemed to have deliberately thrown off all outward writerly stereotypes. She projected herself as an ordinary, middle-class, middle-aged woman and mother doing her best to deal with the day-to-day problems of her own life. She saw no contradiction between being an ordinary woman and being an icon—on the contrary, her unique strength was this self-recognition and her willingness to explore it.

Possibly because I was too young to know better, and also because I've always found the idea that anyone is ordinary hard to believe, I was never totally comfortable with her. Still, we were friendly and mutually respectful; she had also taken the time to read some of my books and speak or write to me very nicely about them (as she did with many young writers). When the opportunity came to interview her I was glad to do so.

At this time in her life Laurence was embroiled in what for her was a terribly painful censorship battle over the teaching of her books in schools. For many people, such a battle would have been strictly about freedom of expression but the accusation that her books were fundamentally immoral cut Laurence, a devout and active Christian, to the quick. The fact the accusers included people in her own community of Lakefield, a small town near Peterborough, Ontario, only made the situation more painful.

Of course I was aware of this situation when I drove up to Lakefield to interview her. The idea was that I would arrive in time for lunch, though her insistence on making lunch for me was over my protests. It seemed to me, as I said, unfair that the "interviewee" should have to double the waste of her time by providing lunch as well as conversation. The bigger truth was that I was afraid the wine that would inevitably accompany lunch would lead to more wine, Scotch, and finally the kind of confessional, sentimental alcoholic-writer scene that generates a pool of misery, regrets and old grudges. Despite my cynicism I was still the fastidious young man hoping there was some graceful way to survive the injustices of the writer's life, and I was afraid the conversation might become uncomfortable.

Naturally I was appalled at my own thoughts. On the appointed day I drove up to Lakefield with a borrowed tape recorder, a lined stenographic pad, and a bottle of Orvieto Classico red.

The woman who answered the door was a frail and shaky version of the Margaret Laurence who had returned to Canada riding the still-swelling crest of her success.

Her handshake was firm, her eyes still fiercely sought mine, but her drinking, the raging battle between her various contradictory selves, and the unpleasant public ordeal to which she had been subjected had all taken their terrible toll. Even as we entered her house I had to offer my arm to steady her, and all the private reservations I'd had—who would ever dare say such a thing aloud?—about her genius having been exaggerated were instantly wiped by the shock of seeing the price that her muse had exacted, and that she had paid.

We first had a cup of coffee and she showed me around the house, including a workroom where she had set out, whether for my benefit or not I couldn't know, a several-hundred-page stack of manuscript she said was her next novel. Later in our visit she talked about how difficult it was for her to write now, after the attacks against her books. I felt she was giving me a double message: the first, her public statement intended for the interview, was that she was just completing her new book; the second, which was up to me to hear but not repeat, was that she had stopped writing fiction.

Feeling tremendously sad, I brought out the wine and we started lunch. She'd made a meat loaf, accompanied by vegetables in the oven, and as I opened the wine she put together a salad. Despite my fears, she hardly drank. She talked about her work for the church, the various articles she had been writing, the Writers' Union and, inevitably and most of all, her public struggles over the banning of her books.

I found it both amazing and terrible that what seemed to me a minor conflict could so take over and distort someone's life. By the time I left her house I felt as though I'd just witnessed a few hours in the martyrdom of someone whose only sin was to be a human being and have inner contradictions.

All this I poured out to Patsy when I got home. Given the somewhat sceptical attitude with which I'd set out that morning, she must have been somewhat surprised to have me return a true believer. That evening, at around nine o'clock, the telephone rang. It was Margaret Laurence, Patsy told me, and I went upstairs to take the call in my office.

What I'd been afraid might happen at lunch seemed to have developed after my departure. Within three seconds it was as if we were back in the bar where our first conversation had taken place. "You know," she confided, "There was one thing I didn't bring up this afternoon. I felt it might be . . . presumptuous . . . and yet it's the most important thing."

As I hastily scribbled notes on the back of whatever bits of papers and old envelopes I could grab, Margaret Laurence explained to me that what she wrote was divinely ordered and inspired and that the voices she heard, while writing, were God's voice.

In fact, that afternoon, voice and dialogue were among the things she had talked about. For her last novel, *The Diviners* (1974), she had been very worried about being able to authentically portray both the states of mind and the actual ways of speaking of people a generation younger than herself. To do so, she said, she had relied heavily on observing and listening to her daughter and her daughter's friends.

I was able to tell her, quite truthfully, that I thought her method must have worked; then I told her about a woman friend who'd brought me the book in a state of flushed enthusiasm saying here, finally, was the first Canadian novel she had ever read that spoke directly to young women and voiced their life experience.

For me, not only because I was a man but for all the other obvious sociological reasons, reading *The Diviners* had not had the same revelatory effect. For me *The Diviners* was not a revelation about my own life but simply a book—more ambitious than *The Stone Angel* in its attempt to portray a generation in change, and perhaps as an inevitable result, more flawed and in places less convincing.

The Diviners typified my whole problem with Canadian literature as a mythology. On the one hand, as a writer who more or less "knew" dozens of other Canadian writers, as well as having close ties to three very different publishing houses of which one was the country's most powerful, I was an apprentice member of what might seem to be the inner circle. On the other hand, the essential Canadian experience—found in Canadian books, the CBC, Pierre Trudeau on certain days, etc.—that essential Canadian whatever that those readers and listeners responded to with "Yes! That's *my* life!" was not, in fact, *my* life.

Aside from the very occasional and unusual novel like *Beautiful Losers*, by Leonard Cohen, or the incredibly alienated stories of Mavis Gallant, Canadian fiction did not open my soul to itself or even remind me of myself. I could enjoy, admire or dismiss Canadian fiction, but I could never expect to discover in it my secret diary. That feeling of self-discovery through books, despite my parents' desperate struggle to assimilate, despite the fact I wore Ernest Hemingway corduroys when I started writing, memorized reams of T.S. Eliot, despite my eager reading of dozens of Canadian novels, was still only going to happen when I read something more self-conscious and twisted, whether it was novels by Nabokov, Freud's absurd confessions, novels I thought of as being "novels of loneliness" by such writers as Camus or Kafka, or even certain British and American writers as uncomfortably isolated with their ambition as a Roman prisoner in a cave with a lion.

There was, in sum, not much I could say in response to her confession of divine inspiration, or to what followed, which was of course an anxious inquiry about whether I found such an idea absurd. As I sat holding the phone and listening to Margaret, the sounds of the rest of the house drifted into my office. We were renting out the ground floor to help pay the mortgage (even though the real estate agent had assured us that we were buying the cheapest house in Toronto) and the usual mid-evening dinner-time chaos prevailed. "I hope I'm not interrupting you," Margaret Laurence said, and I assured her, quite truthfully, that I'd been thinking about her situation ever since leaving her house and that I was glad she had telephoned. I went on with the usual platitudes about how many great writers have felt—is it not in fact the classical tradition?—that they are merely the instruments through which the stories that need to be told are transmitted. That I had felt exactly the same thing—external, if not divine inspiration. I didn't bother mentioning that because even though the ideas for and crucial scenes of many of my novels still appeared to arrive from outside, I had begun to think that whoever was sending them might be picking from the bottom of the heap. In any case, since writing *The Disinherited*, the two novels in which I'd truly felt the power of my own unleashed genius flowing through me, *Wooden Hunters* and *The Colours of War*, had been so flawed and out of focus that I had lost all confidence in my own intuitive judgment about what I was doing, and decided I had to completely retrain myself as a writer, give up simply typing by instinct, and actually apply myself to learning how to write a novel. In fact, some of these thoughts—about the value of giving less place to so-called inspiration and more to learning the craft sufficiently to raise the level of accomplishment—had occurred to me while I was thinking of Margaret Laurence, *The Diviners*, and the many years that had passed between its publication and her partly written new novel. However, how could I, a mere ploughman in the fields of CanLit, speak of such ideas with the reigning queen? Was I going to say to Margaret Laurence that maybe the real reasons her novel was unfinished included technical ones, that perhaps she had to find structural ways to enlarge her fictional scope in order to accommodate the ideas she was now trying to convey? No, I was not.

In the end I thanked her for calling and said how much more I understood how deeply she must be hurt by the controversy now swirling so unfairly around her books. She had been open and generous with me. When I wrote up our interview I mentioned neither the phone call nor my own accompanying thoughts, saying only what she wanted me to say about her new novel: that it was largely written and nearly ready to be published.

As is often the case with such profiles, what got onto the page was a lot less interesting than what actually happened. In the end I committed a basic journalist's sin, and not for the last time. I indirectly allowed the subject of the article to shape and censor what I wrote. However, I don't regret it. What is there to "expose" about someone who has sacrificed herself to her own ideals? In the end, only the fact that she has done so.

And in the meantime, I've often thought about the manuscript she showed me. If it really was a novel-in-progress, and I have never doubted that, I'm glad it hasn't been edited and published in some terribly imperfect form.

By the end of August 1979, I had finished the first draft of *Flowers of Darkness*, the book for which, as Jack McClelland put it, I had gone "to the well one more time."

In the meantime I had spent almost all of the advance I'd received on signing. I was living in the cabin I was in the process of building north of Kingston—I'd spent the previous winter there without power or telephone—and my total current revenues were derived from journalism and the book reviews I was writing for a kind and understanding books editor, Ken Kilpatrick of the *Hamilton Spectator*, who was not only assigning me reviews but getting them reprinted in other newspapers.

One afternoon, sitting on the stairs that led from one section of the cabin to the other, I was calculating the number of feet of two-by-fours I would have to purchase to make the interior wall that was my next step in construction. I also had taken my bank book out of my desk drawer to keep my plans within reason.

To buy the lumber, the gyprock and the other associated materials, I figured would cost me about two hundred dollars. Not so much, except that this paltry sum, as I now saw to my horror, just happened to be my total bank account. I was still owed for a book review, and there was an upcoming journalism assignment for which I could probably get paid in advance, but all things considered, I was broke.

Somehow, things had slid into this situation without my having fully noticed. Just as the inevitable panic and desperation might have started to set in, the telephone rang. It was Dave Godfrey, from the University of Victoria, offering me a one-year position teaching creative writing.

"But the term starts in three weeks," I said.

"We're desperate," he admitted. "But we'd be very glad to have you."

I checked my bank book again. In those days balances were still written out by hand—perhaps the teller's beautiful penmanship had distracted me, and I actually had $2,000, not $200. No, I had read the number correctly.

"I'll be there," I said.

A couple of weeks later I set out on one of those epic drive-my-truck-across-the-country journeys that I'd made at least ten times since the late sixties. I felt weirdly old and crusty to be making this journey again, yet as southern Ontario receded into the distance the old manic and irrational energy of cross-country driving returned, along with the equally manic and irrational hope that having left that old snakeskin behind, I was moving forward into new possibilities.

With me in the truck I had my typewriter, my sound system, and a few suitcases and cardboard boxes of clothes, books and manuscripts. Protecting them from weather and the curious was a hinged plywood top I'd made years before, only slightly rotting but painted with a fresh coat of blue to match my trusty Datsun. Eventually that Datsun would turn into a lacy metallic cheesecloth home for squirrels, parked in front of a maple at my cabin, and finally be towed away, but for this trip it was still ready and willing, so long as I didn't drive too fast.

A few weeks later I had finished another draft of *Flowers of Darkness* and was celebrating with Susan Musgrave and her husband Jeff Greene. Their seaside house was half an hour north of Victoria, and a reliable refuge where good food, excellent companionship and copious amounts of alcohol were combined in a mixture that only Jeff, who happened to be a very successful lawyer specializing in the defence of drunken drivers, could concoct.

It was, as they say, a dark and stormy night. The guest cabin I so frequently occupied was otherwise engaged, which meant, despite the fact I would have Jeff as my lawyer, that taking a walk before driving home was an absolute necessity. Their black Labrador was used to my midnight excursions. Soon we were out on the road, the rain whipping us as we walked along the shore.

The night was so dark, the rain so gusty, the crashing waves so loud, I drifted into thinking about sailing ships stranded in the midst of storms. I'd always been fascinated with the life of Christopher Columbus, and now, for no reason, an idea of Columbus entered my mind. He was pacing a rain-lashed Spanish coast, hoping that somehow he'd procure the money to make his voyage. (Is there a parallel here with getting an advance or a Canada Council grant to write a book?)

And then, as the rain kept on gusting, I forgot about Columbus and found myself thinking about how it must have been to be penniless and without position in the Middle Ages—an absolute nobody on the outside of everything, including being literally outside in the rain and the wind with nowhere to go.

That was when the idea for *The Spanish Doctor* came to me—the story of a medieval Jew crossing Europe to escape persecution, and in search of an enlightenment and age of reason that didn't yet exist. It arrived whole: unbidden, unasked for and finally, because I am too superstitious to easily dismiss such an arrival, unwelcome. For the rest of the walk my mind filled with possible details and currents of the book. By the time I arrived back I was sober. I filed the idea under "ridiculous" and drove home.

Later that fall I had to go to Toronto to discuss the editing of *Flowers of Darkness*. While there I had lunch with Anna Porter to discuss both that novel—she had been reading the various drafts from the beginning—and plans for the paperback edition of *Kitty Malone*.

As always, Anna had her eye on the future and was more interested in the next book I might write than in the book already written.

I explained to her that I was sure that *Flowers of Darkness* would be the last of my rural novels, and that I needed to make some kind of break with what I'd been doing.

"What did you have in mind?" she asked.

"I've been writing some short stories."

"Short stories," she said, as though someone had just given her fried eggs for Christmas.

I knew what she meant. Paperback publishers might like to read short stories, but they didn't line up to publish them. Anna stared down into her wine glass the way she always did when preparing to give me a lecture. It was exactly the same gesture that had preceded her saying to me, about *The Colours of War*, "Look, Cohen, I've read this manuscript twice and all I can say is that it's either a work of complete genius or a total disaster."

"Look, Cohen," Anna now said. "I can understand why you're tired of these rural novels. Although I love them, as you know. And if you want to write more of them I'd be glad to publish them. As you know. But why don't you write something that reveals more about yourself? Your books are always so distant. Why don't you write something about being Jewish? You know what I think? I think you're afraid to write about being Jewish and what it means to you."

This was not an entirely new theme. Anna had often told me I should write fiction that was more personal and more Jewish. I would reply that my life was boring for confessional writing and in any case I was too young and innocent to have anything to confess. So far as being Jewish went, my stock response was that I was from Ottawa and had stopped going to synagogue on my bar mitzvah.

Nonetheless, I knew what she was getting at. An immigrant and outsider herself, she knew I wasn't born in Rosedale and that my sensibility, whatever it was, certainly hadn't come from either downtown Toronto or agricultural Canada.

"Okay," I said, staring into my own glass of wine. It was empty. "Surprise. I did have an idea for a novel with a Jew in it. But I need more wine to tell you about it."

With the help of a compliant waiter, I began on the story of the medieval Spanish doctor. In the almost ten years I'd known Anna, I'd probably told her ideas for over a dozen novels, many of them invented as I spoke. This one had no further purpose than to justify more free wine and, possibly, by its very absurdity, to get her to stop telling me to write about being Jewish.

Meanwhile, however, as I described the life of this doctor—I'd now given him a name, Avram Halevi—Anna listened with a total fascination I'd never quite experienced.

"Fantastic!" she said when I was finished. "What an idea. Do it."

"Just the research would cost a fortune," I objected. "And no one will want to read it."

"I do," she said. "How much do you need?"

Mindful that at the end of the academic year I would be out of a job and money again, and wanting to put an end to the conversation, I said, "Twenty-five thousand dollars."

"Done," she said. "Give me a sample chapter and an outline."

When Charles Dickens went to America, adoring crowds lined up outside his hotel hoping for an autograph. He was so energized by this mass display of love that during the day, as his coach proceeded from town to town, he would leap out and walk with the horses for hours at a time, dragging them along and exhausting all those around him.

When Byron visited Venice he swam from the Lido across the lagoon and up the Grand Canal. This took four hours and the two companions he'd started out with had to be fished from the water by a rescue gondola.

When I went to Spain, I performed no athletic feats, signed no autographs, and was completely unsuccessful at writing anything Byron or Dickens would have wanted to find on their desks. Such are the limitations of travel.

Patsy had agreed to come with me. She had thrown her full support behind the project, though neither of us knew quite how extensive that support would have to be. (I ended up doing most of the writing of this voluminous novel when our first child was still an infant). Having her with me in Spain was both psychologically important and extremely useful, since she was a native Spanish speaker and already knew the country well.

It was late August when we arrived, and the airport was predictably hot and dusty. We went to our hotel, then walked out onto the streets of Madrid.

My first shock: everyone I saw looked exactly like me! Slightly shorter than they were supposed to be, with sallow skin, horn-rimmed glasses and clothes that didn't match—but it was more than that, it was something in the combination of being both extrovert and furtive, timorous and overconfident, night creatures at large during the day. Suddenly I knew, with a conviction that has never left me, that I was in the land of my ancestors.

In our century writers may be unread but are seldom untravelled. Although I'd already noticed that I wasn't Dickens or Byron, I'd visited many countries, always enjoyed them, sometimes learned something about them, but always felt, naturally, like an outsider, even if well tolerated. It's just like being in Canada, I would say to myself in explanation of why I found travelling so easy.

But this was different. Even though I knew nothing about Spain I felt like an insider right away. The sensation continued when we went to visit the Prado. Of course, I had seen illustrations of many of the paintings on display there, and perhaps that was why it seemed so eerily familiar.

After a couple of days in Madrid we went south to Toledo. This was to be the first physical locale for my novel. Originally I'd thought of setting it at the time of Columbus's first voyage to America; modern Spain's first two great historically significant acts had been to send Columbus in one direction and its Jews in another, and the irony was very tempting.

But I had discovered that the expulsion of the Jews from Spain was only the final step in a process that began with the first great wave of the Black Death in 1348. Predictably, the Jews were blamed for this plague except in Castile, of which Toledo was the capital. In Castile there were as many as three hundred separate Jewish communities living under the protection of the King. The Jews of Castile supported numerous universities and centres of study. In other cities throughout Aragon, Portugal and Navarre, there were other such centres of learning. For Jewish civilization in Europe these were the last moments of a never-to-be-repeated golden era when Spanish Jews lived in harmony with Arabs and Christians.

When Pedro of Castile (also known as Pedro the Cruel) was challenged in 1369, the Jews sided with him because he had been their patron. When he was overthrown, things began to go downhill. In 1391, beginning with a massacre in Seville, Jewish settlements and ghettos were attacked all over the Iberian Peninsula, from the Pyrenees to the Straits of Gibraltar. Tens of thousands of Jews died and tens of thousands more converted. These converts, known as conversos or marranos, eventually became common targets for the Inquisition.

The destruction of Spanish Jewry through the Inquisition and the expulsion was the most tragic event in Jewish history until the Second World War. I set the novel in Toledo, at the moment when it had just became apparent that this destruction was inevitable.

Another advantage of the city was its state of historical preservation. I (along with the tens of thousands of tourists who visited it daily) was assured of finding in it a reasonably authentic version of what Toledo looked like in the fourteenth century.

We arranged to stay in a hotel that had once been a cardinal's palace. This seemed appropriate, since such a cardinal had an important though villainous role to play in my hypothetical novel. (I could be reasonably certain that there were no hotels that had formerly been the palatial residences of rich and famous Jews—curiously enough, Toledo is not the only city I've visited that has no such hotels. But that would be a different travel story.)

The cardinal's palace was suitably opulent, as well as being provided with a restaurant splendid in every respect save that Patsy got violently ill both times we ate there. As advertised, the city was a well-kept version of what, for all I knew, it had been in the Middle Ages. A small, densely populated walled city set on a series of cliffs and divided into various districts that could be separated by iron gates, Toledo has an undeniable beauty and magic, despite the throngs of tourists, that invites the visitor to fill that emptiness with the visions of his or her own imagination.

The former Jewish presence in Toledo was duly mentioned in various guidebooks, and there was even a very ancient synagogue to be seen (which had later been converted into a church and then reconverted into a synagogue). The day I went to see it happened to be Yom Kippur, and the synagogue was closed. When I asked why, I was told a German film crew was inside, setting up for a television special on the historic past of Spain's Jews. This led to a vigorous discussion during which Patsy relied on many words not to be found in Berlitz dictionaries. After we were allowed in I asked if the Jews of Toledo ever worshipped here and I was told that although the city did have some Jewish families, regrettably very few, they didn't use the synagogue.

There was a restaurant up the hill from the hotel, a modest place with a terrific view of the plains below, plains on which medieval fairs had been set up, and towards which the Jews of Toledo had tried to flee, most of them unsuccessfully, when their barrio was invaded and set on fire in 1391.

One night at this friendly and affordable restaurant, which specialized in lunches because most of the tourist buses left in the late afternoon for Madrid—only two hours away—I realized my project was ridiculous. Toledo was a sort of medieval Disneyland, where we were dutifully making the rounds of churches, synagogues, old Roman arenas, paintings, houses of former illustrious citizens, etc. I proposed that we cut our losses, and set out for the north, taking advantage of being in Spain to see as much as possible.

That night I dreamed the first section of my novel. When I woke up in the morning and went outside, I saw not the prettily restored buildings but the dry stony soil, the bushes that would have torn at your skin as you slid to escape, the claustrophobic architecture of a city designed to be ruled by fear.

We spent ten days driving around Spain, then returned to Toledo. Everything I saw in the present had become a thin contemporary transparency laid over a landscape from which, hour by hour, I was learning to subtract the centuries.

By the time we left Toledo a second time, and were spending our last night in Madrid before flying home, I had filled pages with notes, could speak rudimentary Spanish, and had bought the books I would need for my research. But now when I looked at the people on the streets of Madrid they were utter strangers. I was no longer inside them. Instead, I was in the nightmare their ancestors and mine had shared, the nightmare that for some had ended in death and exile, for others in the beginnings of a new and dazzling empire.

My first conception of *The Spanish Doctor* had been entirely as a historical novel, but in the early drafts I experimented with linking it to the present, by having a present-day narrator who in investigating the background of his grandfather stumbled across a much earlier story of his own ancestors. As might have been predicted, the older story overwhelmed the story of his own life. In the end I cut the contemporary sections free, and kept them to use in other fiction, because by then I was involved in the lives of these twentieth-century characters. One, Tomas Benares, became the protagonist of a story called "The Sins of Tomas Benares," which ended up, along with another rescued fragment, "Sentimental Meetings," in my collection *Café Le Dog*. Strangely enough, as illegitimate as it may seem to recycle unusable novel fragments as short stories, these two stories did very well and have gone on to enjoy completely independent lives in numerous anthologies and translations.

But even having separated these stories, the present-day versions of these families continued to obsess me, and they became the basis of my two following novels, *Nadine* (1986) and *Emotional Arithmetic* (1990). Historically, literarily and emotionally they form a unity with *The Spanish Doctor*, a multi-century triptych that I see as a single work. Like the stories, however, they have been regarded as completely separate by critics, readers and even their publishers. It is odd to think that, had I given them a label (as I purposely did the Salem novels) in order to draw attention to their commonalities, that label would probably have caused the three books to be seen in an entirely different light. As it is, a project that occupied me for almost a decade has more or less entirely disappeared from sight, although the individual books still find some readers.

Perhaps this goes to show that every written work has the right to find its own way to oblivion. Or it could be that the real reason for this disappearance relative to my other books is not a public-relations failure, but that the novels are without merit. In any case, their failure in Canada, especially in contrast with the success of the novels that came before and after them, has often made me think about the conversation I had with Anna Porter twenty years ago, when she accused me of being afraid to explore my Jewishness and what it meant to me.

Whether I was or should have been afraid to explore that territory or write the books, I don't know. But had I known the reception they would have in Canada, I certainly would have been afraid to publish them.

On the positive side, the novels succeeded in the U.S., the U.K. and in translation, both critically and commercially, in inverse relation to their Canadian critical reception.

The negative side was their reception here. *The Spanish Doctor* and *Nadine* were especially torn to pieces by the Canadian critics. I was accused of deserting my Canadian muse by daring to set books outside the country, not doing my research, selling out my literary talents and deliberately writing mass market products to make money, exploiting female sensibility by writing from the female point of view, etc. *Emotional Arithmetic* received more favourable treatment, but unfortunately its publisher was busy going bankrupt the season it was released.

My reaction to all this was undoubtedly intensified by the fact that the publication day of *The Spanish Doctor*, when it received its most scathing reviews, was the day after my father died unexpectedly of a stroke.

For over a decade my father had been ill with myasthenia, a disease involving failure of the autonomous nervous system, e.g., breathing and swallowing. For the first years he was often hospitalized and on the brink of death. However, a new drug that turned out to be a miracle cure, at least for him, had put him into remission and back on his feet. It had also confirmed his faith in the mightiness of science and sent him back to work at the National Research

Council and even to the golf course where, he would claim, he was playing better than ever.

He died at seventy, having achieved his biblical due, and happily his death was instantaneous; he did not have to repeat the decline into protracted debility and illness that he had already experienced. Nonetheless, I was hit hard by it, and the fact that my own career imploded at the same time didn't help.

My response to these events was to want to escape. But I had agreed to be chairman of the Writers' Union, and could not, in conscience, withdraw from the obligation. The work with the union provided its own distractions and rewards, but it was bizarre to be toiling at the very centre of Canadian cultural nationalism at a time when I would have been most pleased to avoid the public eye, when I felt I was being chastised for having dared to write about foreign Jews, instead of long-time Canadians who might once have been immigrants fleeing disagreeable situations, but had been transformed by history into founding fathers and chief ancestors.

When, partway through the year, Patsy became pregnant with our daughter Madeleine and suggested we might spend her maternity leave in Paris, I was quick to agree. I still treasure the memorable moment when she came out with this amazing proposition. We were in the kitchen preparing supper. I was opening a bottle of wine (long afterwards, Patsy told me that following my father's death I stayed drunk for two years, an accusation I deny). As it happened we had Canadian friends in Paris, and within the next month I was in France checking out various apartments we could lease.

Over the next decade, I would spend almost half my time in France, and during that period my own personal re-education, which had begun with my research trips for *The Spanish Doctor,* continued. As both writer and reader I was gratefully experiencing a tremendous widening of horizons and possibilities. I had a new language, new literatures, new audiences, new publishers and translators, new territories to explore. Along the way I learned how to translate, an activity that has offered me an unmatchable window into both Quebec literature and the intricacies of another language. The feeling I had at the end of the seventies, that writing another book meant going back to an exhausted well, was never to return.

During that period when my own literary vistas and ambitions were changing and broadening, so did the cultural context from which I was so eagerly freeing myself.

By now, the old CanLit scene, so vigorously roasted by so many throughout the eighties, has both evolved and, in many ways, shrunk beyond recognition. The networks of critics that once supported and shaped it are no longer visible; and the academic CanLit industry has been drastically downsized, as have so many Canadian industries.

At the same time the selling and publishing of books has been transformed. Many of the independent bookstores whose owners and staff literally campaigned for Canadian books, hand-sold them to their initially dubious customers, provided venues for hundreds and thousands of readings and were the foundation of the market for Canadian-authored books have gone out of business or been bought by the chains. A single chain, Chapters, is now estimated to sell over fifty per cent of all Canadian books.

At the same time, many publishing houses that were absolutely crucial twenty and thirty years ago have gone bankrupt or got out of the business of publishing culturally important books—among the more obvious are Clarke, Irwin and Macmillan. McClelland & Stewart still publishes many key books, but has reduced its list. Formerly independent small publishers such as Anansi and Cormorant are now virtual imprints of much larger companies; foreign-owned publishers have become important players, and their Canadian lists often as significant as those of their Canadian rivals.

Changed, too, is the nature of the books that succeed in Canada and the extent of their success. In fiction, aside from a few long-standing, big-name authors, many of the huge successes of the last ten years have been first novels, with Canadian sales sometimes exceeding a hundred thousand copies. Equally refreshing is that the content of these novels have been diverse and unpredictable in every way. Canadian fiction has not only broken out at home in the sense of extending its boundaries, it has also done extraordinarily well abroad, both commercially and in terms of winning important prizes. CanLit as it once was may have shrunk, but the books being published in Canada by Canadians are of an unprecedented variety and range, and have had amazing success in reaching out to all sorts of readers both at home and all over the world.

Does this mean everything has come up roses for Canada's writers? Alas, no. While it is true that there are a few books pulling in huge sales and advances, the vast majority are published in a fragmented market that has seen high school and university sales diminish while the so-called general readership has divided itself up into readers interested only in a given region or gender or topic or aesthetic approach. The readers who at the height of political Canadian nationalism were attracted by the simple fact that a book (or a movie or a political idea) was Canadian have disappeared. There may be four or five successful books a year that sell ten times as much as they used to, but it is as difficult as ever for a hardcover novel to end up selling (after returns) two thousand copies.

The paperback industry has also been totally transformed, and the news for writers is bad. In fiction, the mass-market editions that sold for a few dollars have largely been replaced by trade paperbacks that sell for fifteen to twenty dollars. This has worked well for publishers, who can now break even on a trade edition that sells three thousand copies. But compared to the ten or twenty thousand copies the mass-market editions sold, it represents a sharp drop in the number of readers a modestly popular writer of fiction can expect, even for a relatively successful book.

A beginning writer today is faced with an intimidating situation. On the one hand there is the tantalizing vista of megapublishers, international financial bonanzas and instant world fame. The more probable outcome, however, is a book published by a small press and reaching its (small) audience through incessant readings and public appearances, rather than the ever-diminishing and ever-more-marginalized possibilities offered by newspapers, radio and television.

Worse yet, Canadian writers live in a country that is busily starving its libraries, its schools, its universities and its research institutions. Every aspect of intellectual life is under attack, which doesn't make a good environment for books, although conversely (or perversely), in such a situation anything is possible. Writers and thinkers often have the greatest freedom at times when no one seems to be listening.

Some people have argued that the reason so many Canadian books don't do well is that so many of them are subsidized by government grants, which encourage mediocrity. If only! The truth is that government grants for publishing and writing have been steadily cut back over the last twenty years or so. The maximum writing grant from the Canada Council is now just over half of what it used to be. Does that mean that books written on such grants are almost twice as good? Publishers receive a much smaller portion of their budgets in grants than they did fifteen years ago. Does that mean they have become more expert in predicting and publishing what will sell?

The reality is that publishing in every Western country, no matter what its level of government support, is under similar stresses. The business trend to mergers and internationalization applies in the U.S., Britain, Scandinavia and the Netherlands just as much as it does here, and the trend is everywhere accompanied by the same problems.

What does all this mean for a middle-aged writer with half or more of his books behind him? In all, not much. As always, each book is an adventure. It starts off as an idea that somehow survives getting forgotten or thrown in the wastebasket. I'm pickier than I used to be about what

books I will write, so most often the writing itself is as fulfilling and challenging an occupation as I could hope for.
Yet some things are the same as they always were: until a
book is actually published, I still can't be sure it will ever
see the light of day nor can I predict either its public fate
or the way I myself will feel about it. In the end, though
things are a bit better, nothing has really changed. I am
always writing whatever book I am writing because it so
absorbs me I can't do anything else. A closed circle that
offers no further explanation.

Last Seen
and After

----

personal necessity is personal
this time...accumulated effect
of all these deaths, including
possibly the deaths of my ideas
about writing and of self

hen I started writing this memoir, I was curious to know what narrator would invent himself, what story he would tell and through what kind of lens he would view the past. Also: would that lens stay the same? It's one thing to look back at events that occurred several decades ago and have been covered up or perhaps even resolved. But the closer one draws to the present, the less time there has been for events to rearrange themselves into a benevolent and sentimental story with a happy ending.

Like most writers, I have often played with the idea of writing some sort of account of my life. *The Grievances*, I sometimes thought I would call it, or, even better, *The Injustices*. Perhaps it would be a total parody along the lines of *Portrait of the Artist as a Young Dog*. Or I could imitate *That Summer in Paris*: my version would be *That Summer in Toronto* and I would give a comical representation of the Coach House and Anansi crowds as would-be Bloomsbury Groups, on the fringes of which I, the perfect innocent, would make my worshipful observations. Instead of scenes of boxing with Hemingway, I would describe (fictional) dope-smoking contests with well-known Canadian writers. I had plenty of material.

So a few years ago, when Anne Collins (then executive editor of *Toronto Life*) asked me for a memoir-type piece about 1966, I thought of all these failed attempts, but agreed to try. As it turned out, writing about 1966 in Toronto was both easy and enjoyable, since it didn't involve either of the two most obvious autobiographical subjects: my childhood and my life as a writer.

When Anne was reincarnated as a book publisher, it was natural enough for her to suggest that the magazine piece might reincarnate itself as a book. I had serious reservations. First, my life has not been one of swash-buckling adventure, incident and excitement. If I couldn't find it interesting, how could a reader? Second, in my few stabs at autobiographical writing, I usually cast myself as the anti-heroic buffoon stumbling through the lives of my betters. Sitting at the typewriter or computer I would pound away for a few hours, chortling at the absurdity of it all. Then I would go for a walk, come back, read what I'd written and throw it out. Nonetheless, I decided to make one more try, because since my last attempts one very important thing had changed: my view of my own past.

A dozen years ago, I was in what is now called "mid-career": I had written a lot of books and was over forty years old. So far as a career went, however, I didn't have one. My personal life, with a fulfilling relationship, four children and everything stimulating about spending a lot of time abroad, was great, but my so-called professional existence was in a tailspin that ended in a total crash.

In the previous chapter I summed up the whole period occupied by the writing and publication of *The Spanish Doctor, Nadine* and *Emotional Arithmetic* with the comment that if had I known what their reception in Canada would be like, I would have been afraid to publish them. I noted, too, that despite the Canadian reaction, the novels had done well abroad. This version of events, while true, is not the whole truth, nor is it what I thought I was going through at the time.

After Anna Porter and then Jack McClelland left McClelland & Stewart, I accepted an offer from Penguin Books to publish *Nadine* with them. Though the new regime at M&S was still friendly to me, my motivation for moving was the usual: the prospect of more money and a larger audience. In the short run, the decision seemed to work out. Penguin had published the paperback of *The Spanish Doctor* with great success—in England as well as in Canada; and shortly after they signed up *Nadine*, Viking/Penguin in London made an offer for British rights. A couple of translation sales followed, and by the beginning of the year in Paris I no longer cared so much about *The Spanish Doctor*'s scathing reception in Canada, because I had begun to see myself as on my way to having a veritable empire of countries in which my books would be eagerly devoured.

Then came the actual publication of *Nadine*—and with it double disaster. Just before publication day it was discovered that the printed book had a serious error: there was a place where several paragraphs had been repeated and others left out. Penguin, eager for a flawless launch, called back the entire printing from bookstores to replace it with

a corrected version. As it turned out, *Nadine* was destined
to be doubly shredded. Aside from the physical problems
there was a disastrous review in *The Globe and Mail*, the
country's most influential newspaper. The reviewer found
every aspect of the book completely lacking in merit, and
accused me of having written an unconvincing monstros-
ity that, among its many other sins, dared to tell part of the
story from the point of view of a woman. It was also written, according to the reviewer, in a pulp-fiction mass-
market style, in order to make money. The review took up
an enormous amount of space and featured a large picture
of the unfortunate author. Much of the promotion planned
for the book then melted away, and what was supposed to
be my "break-out book" turned into a rather large nail in
the coffin of my Canadian literary reputation. It seemed
obvious that I was absolutely finished. In 1981 *Flowers of
Darkness* had been received with a polite lack of enthusiasm. In 1984 *The Spanish Doctor* had been definitively
roasted. Now *Nadine* was getting the same treatment. By
the time I got back to France after two weeks of criss-
crossing the country trying to counter the effects of the
one review everyone had read, and trying to explain to
bookstores why their copies of my book were now in
limbo, it seemed to me that no novel I could write would
ever get me out of the hole I'd been placed in. Yet writing a
novel, in fact a companion novel to *Nadine*, was exactly the
project I was engaged in.

Bad though my professional situation was, there was
also a separate reality: I was in Paris for a year with my
family, free to write or do anything I pleased. Soon Canada
began to seem very far away. I worked on some zany short

stories (which ended up getting published in French translation long before I could find an English-language publisher), fiddled about with the novel and produced a disorganized first draft that was at least a pile of paper, though its confusion reflected my own uncertainty about what I was doing and my growing loss of confidence. Nonetheless, we had a great time in France and I assumed that on my return to Canada I would be able to straighten out my situation.

Unfortunately, coming back only confirmed my earlier fears. I found that the invitations I used to get to give lectures and readings, or to speak on CBC-Radio, etc., were no longer forthcoming. It was as though I'd been away a decade, not a year. And the novel I was working on—*Emotional Arithmetic*—seemed not only confused, but directionless. I struggled for many months to get it into shape, but when my agent passed it on to Penguin, the publisher—Cynthia Good—suggested that I cut everything after the first fifteen pages. "But," I objected, "that's most of the novel and most of the characters."

"I know," she said. "But I don't think readers would be interested in those people."

Shocked and furious, so upset I was unable to speak, I stalked out. But by the time I got to the parking lot I had seen a silver lining. Almost every publisher in Toronto had tried to buy *Nadine* when it was auctioned. I would have my agent auction off *Emotional Arithmetic*, make a pile of money and end up with the last laugh.

The next week my agent sent the novel out to five publishers. Within a few weeks four of them had responded. The fifth was well known for not bothering to read the manuscripts it received. All four responses were declines. The verdict was surprisingly unanimous—all agreed the novel had some (but not too many) strengths, was totally unsaleable because it was about old people and the Holocaust (both boring subjects), and added that although I was a nice fellow and very likeable I was now myself too old and out of date to be of interest to the reading public.

"Old! Fifteen minutes ago I was the young rising star."

"It wasn't fifteen minutes," my agent said gently. "It's been almost ten years."

So, there I was. Forty-five years old and totally washed up. I wasn't necessarily about to starve. For projects I wrote under other people's names, or translations I did of other people's books, there was a reasonably healthy demand. Otherwise I was the hockey player who'd always been on the verge of having that one great season, only to find that suddenly both his knees are gone and that if he wants to travel even on a minor league bus he will have to buy his own ticket.

Eventually, two publishers—Anna Porter and Scott McIntyre, both inheritors of the M&S creed of absolute loyalty to the author—found out about my predicament and with tremendous generosity, because neither of them was publishing fiction at the time, offered to take on *Emotional Arithmetic*. Of course I couldn't saddle them with this money-losing proposition, but their gestures made me feel a lot better. Then finally the publisher who'd never responded, Lester & Orpen Dennys, got around to reading the novel and made an offer. It wasn't a lot of money (just a fraction of what Penguin had paid for *Nadine*) but I was more than grateful. Even when they were shut down during my tour I considered it only a minor inconvenience compared to what had been happening. What it meant, though, was that while I was on the road promoting the book, bookstores were packing up their copies and shipping them to the warehouse as fast as they could to make sure they got their money back, while it was still possible, for copies that might have been unsold had they kept them in the store. As it turned out, I was right to take this horrible development in stride, because my association with Louise Dennys was the beginning of a publishing relationship that has allowed me to write my best books.

In the summer of 1991, to my great relief, we returned to France for another year-long stay, this time in the south, in a small village north of Avignon. I had with me manuscripts-in-progress for two novels. One was *Elizabeth and After*—after five years I was still working away on it. The other, which would become *The Bookseller*, was based on two brothers who had started out in *Elizabeth and After* but then caused so many problems I'd cut them out and sent them to Toronto to be in their own book.

In October I went to Amsterdam to do publicity for the Dutch translation of *Emotional Arithmetic*. My Dutch publisher, Ivo Gay, was one of those publishers any writer would be lucky to have. The first of my books he had published was *The Spanish Doctor*, which he decided to acquire within forty-eight hours of receiving it. The book was a tremendous success in Holland, both critically and commercially, so much so that in the years that followed I was sometimes recognized on the street or in bookstores. But what was equally interesting to me about its reception was that it was read not as a descent into some lower form of writing, but as a literary work with its own formal originality that approached the medieval period in an entirely unique way. Aside from my finding this kind of reading flattering, it also happened to coincide with my intentions in writing the book.

Of course I had been afraid that *Nadine*, set in the present, would not appeal to Ivo because it lacked the commercial appeal of historical fiction. I shouldn't have worried. True, the book didn't sell well, but fortunately for me Ivo belonged to that small but treasured group of publishers, the your-latest-is-your-greatest school. Not only that, but being himself a Belgian Jew who'd established himself in the competitive and exclusive world of Dutch publishing, he was a double outsider for whom the idea of a Canadian writing about Europe was neither preposterous nor audacious. In fact, he was of the opinion that those who view things from the outside have the advantage of being free of the cultural and intellectual blinders often worn by those whose whole lives have been lived on the inside.

This is obviously the opposite of the prevalent Canadian belief that one can write effectively and authentically only about what one actually is, and that all good writing comes out of one's "authentic" situation, i.e., one's sociologically and historically described self.

There are huge problems with that idea, aside from the question of whether such a thing as "authenticity" can be said to exist. Some people with good personal and historical justification can and do regard themselves as, say, authentically a member of a certain racial or ethnic community, or authentically rooted in a piece of ground tilled by the same family for nine generations, or authentically a *pure laine* Quebecker, etc., but many others cannot. For those of mixed geographic/racial/ethnic, etc., ancestry, to say nothing of self-declared free spirits or even those who see no reason why the unsupported habits and assumptions of the past should have more power to define them than the ideas they choose to adhere to, claiming such an affiliation is impossible, or at least entirely fictional.

In fact, it has often seemed to me that the whole idea of authenticity is just a way for some groups of people to exclude or brand inferior everyone not in their group.

What does all this sociology have to do with the life and direction of the imagination? A lot.

After all, the "imagination" is not something that floats around in people's heads like an unattached genie. And even though it may be fashionable and amusing to talk about left-brain and right-brain thinking, as though a person's so-called creative and analytic faculties were like two strangers who have never shaken hands, I'm convinced that there are intimate ties between what people propose to themselves as their so-called rational thoughts and what they imagine. Observing myself, my colleagues and the hundreds of writers I've encountered in creative writing classes and as writer-in-residence, it has become obvious to me that there is a very close relationship between what people believe or think they can write, what they, analytically, think writing is, and what they in the end do write.

Of course, one of the most difficult things in writing is to discover what one is taking for granted. The strange thing about blinders is that they are invisible to the wearer, until something unexpected happens.

On the second night of my stay, I was in my hotel reading a magazine, when the telephone rang. It was my brother Andy, and he was calling to inform me he had terminal cancer. For reasons I have never entirely understood, this news—and what followed—shattered me in a way from which I cannot imagine ever completely recovering.

Even now, faced with my own demise, I have had a hard time moving out of the shadow of his, as though in my eyes that particular death somehow stood for all deaths, including my own.

Strangely enough, at the time Andy called I had just— that very week—finished writing the first draft of *The Bookseller*, a novel in which a relatively stable and sedate younger brother (although he has his own problems) attempts to save the life of his hopelessly weak and indebted older brother. Naturally, when I was working on the novel I had thought how amusing my own brother would find this inside-out view of things, since he was younger and, at least apparently, much more stable and sedate than I had ever been. And I looked forward to showing him this novel, certain he would enjoy the parodic take on us and our family.

Later I wondered if writing this novel had been an expression of some mysterious unconscious knowledge that something was terribly wrong with Andy. My sister-in-law also told me about various ominous foreshadowings. One after another, I remembered all sorts of banal incidents that, strung together, should have set off alarms. But they didn't. I was utterly unprepared for his call, and when I set down the phone I only knew that I'd been pushed across a boundary that would forever separate me from the life I'd previously lived.

About six months after my brother's death—a long and horrible process—I was driving home from my cabin to Toronto when I got stuck in slow-moving traffic outside Oshawa. I began to daydream that I was in Toronto already, out of my car and walking down Queen Street near Spadina. It was early November; the trees by the highway still had a scattering of leaves and the sky was an iron grey barely enlivened by faint patches of pale blue.

I saw myself going into a bar, finding a table at the back, and ordering a beer. I was tired. The process of my brother's illness and death had exhausted and demoralized me so totally that the prospect of sitting at the back of some dark anonymous bar, removed from every attachment and obligation, could not have been more attractive. I pictured myself sitting there, finally at ease, watching a chorus line of beerily drunken men doing a kick dance at the front of the bar in rhythm to the singing of a greasy imitation Elvis. *Perfect*, I thought. And then, looking more closely at the men, I saw that one of them looked exactly like Andy.

For the next hour this scenario continued to unfold and elaborate itself. I suppose it was one of those strange post-death encounters one reads about in the papers—in any case, I felt as though I had actually seen my brother again, as though I'd met him in some alternative world in which he'd mysteriously survived or reappeared. The feeling was a good one. For the first time since the day he'd called me in Amsterdam, I felt truly relaxed and whole.

It was the fall of 1992. The novel I'd never gotten to show him, *The Bookseller*, was finished and entering production for publication the next spring. Officially, at least to myself, I was working on *Elizabeth and After*, by now a mountain of files and drafts still in search of whatever it was that would pull the whole thing together. In truth, however, I wasn't really working at all. The world of books had come to seem entirely artificial and contrived, and books themselves optimistic little fairy tales that couldn't touch or contain what I was going through. Every day I sat down to work on my novel but, so far as I was concerned, I might as well have been building a ship out of toothpicks.

When I got home I piled up the file folders and shoved them into a drawer. My desk looked better clean.

Over the next few days I began writing down the strange waking dream I'd had. I didn't think of it as something to publish. There was no possible frame or structure, it was just something I was writing down. But I liked writing it—it brought back the feeling of wholeness I'd experienced at the time, and so I kept working on it for about a month, until I had a fifty-page fragment, not a novel or a book in the normal sense because it lacked the usual boundaries between writer and narrator, page and reader, story and autobiography. When I was finished I filed it away, happy to have written it but with no further plans, and went on grinding out a living by doing some translating, which, since I was paid by the word, seemed to me the most candid of occupations. Eventually the fragment would turn into what I ended up calling a novel, *Last*

Seen. But it was a novel different from any of my other novels. For most of its writing I had no intention of publishing it, and even when I finally admitted to myself that this pile of pages was actually a book-in-progress, I still didn't care what people would think of it or how it would be received. I wrote it because I was a writer and that was what I did when something happened—I wrote. And I was still so obsessed with Andy's death that I really couldn't think or write about anything else. When it was finally finished it had become a strange amalgam of naked autobiography and improbable fantasy, and part of what had been broken was healed. The rest I would live with.

In August 1995 we returned to France for what we knew would be our final year there for a while, because after this our son Daniel would be too close to the end of high school to spend a year out of the country. *Last Seen* was by now in an advanced draft, though there was still some final polishing to do and it wasn't scheduled for publication until fall '96. As we packed to leave Toronto I remembered that there was still that old unfinished novel I'd never quite given up on, *Elizabeth and After*, and at the last minute I threw the folders into a briefcase. By now some of them had taken on a prehistoric look. The original coffee stains were getting towards being ten years old. Some of the files were labelled by the names of their main characters. Others were called things like "obsolete drafts" or "possibilities." All in all there were several hundred pages. The prospect of opening the folders and actually reading them made me queasy.

When we got to France, just the sight of the briefcase was enough to bring back the queasy feeling, and after setting *Last Seen* in the centre of my work table, I took the *Elizabeth* briefcase and shoved it deep into the clothes closet under a pile of running shoes and tennis equipment.

During our previous year here I had spent an enormous amount of time and emotional energy worrying about my brother and planning my next trip back to Ottawa to see him. One of the things I loved to do was go for runs. In the winter there are a few days when the mistral is overpowering, but otherwise, running is a year-round activity, and every second morning or so I would run for about an hour along the roads that seamed the hills surrounding our village.

The last time, on these runs, I had found myself breathing the mantra "Andy *live*, Andy *live*, Andy *live*" with every stride. Now it was too late. The mantra hadn't worked. It was just me again, panting and gasping with no higher purpose than to catch the heartbreakingly spectacular view I knew was always waiting for me around the next corner.

Nonetheless, I was very glad to be here. France had graduated from being an escape from Canada to being an alternative existence in which my job was to play the happy tourist. It wasn't hard. Free from the distractions and obligations of life in the place where I really lived, I found it easy to focus on my writing for a few hours each day, yet still have lots of time and energy left over for driving around the countryside, searching out terrific cheap restaurants and socializing with the friends we'd made over the years, who were even more obsessed with—and expert in—the pleasures of eating and drinking than we were.

In Canada such an existence would seem frivolous. In France it was normal. Even being a writer is normal, and actually highly respected. France is a country that worships language above all other gods, and moreover takes the printed word as its highest manifestation.

Being a writer, and even better, a writer who could show a few books that had been translated from my own barbarian tongue into French itself, I was immediately granted a place in an aristocracy so important it almost overcame the set of prejudices usually directed towards foreigners. Patsy, being a publisher, was granted even higher status, and when she helped our village school put together a book of the children's writings, her status as local saint and *patronne* was firmly established.

Another huge benefit of France being so oriented towards print is the print itself: interesting newspapers, piles of magazines, French literature. Each time we came for a year to France I tried to read at least a handful of the year's most prominent literary books. I found them fascinating, but whenever I was among professional acquaintances in Paris—publishers, agents, etc.—they always claimed to find anything written recently in France flat, lifeless and entirely lacking compared with whatever obscure American writer had lately become the latest *must* fashion in literary Paris. "Our writers have completely lost touch," they would complain. "They don't sell anywhere. Not here, not abroad."

It's true that French literature isn't very prominent in North America now compared to its status in the post-war period when Sartre, Camus and de Beauvoir were practically household names here. French literary critics like to attribute this decline to their contemporary writers not being very good. But it seems to me that this is just another volley in the usual critic-writer war, because the truth is that North America has become so self-obsessed, and American publishing so relentlessly commercial, that aside from a brief flurry of interest in so-called magic realism, translated books have had only a tiny place in American publishing for the past thirty years. French writers may have their ups and downs, but for a country to measure the worth of its writers by their success in foreign markets is to ignore the real meaning of globalization in publishing, which is that the foreign markets (i.e., North America, in this case) just aren't interested in publishing translated French books, because it is more profitable to publish and promote a small number of titles, each of which sells a lot, than to try to publish and promote a large number of titles that will sell only a few thousand copies each. Given this reality, the best thing French writers could do to make themselves "better" writers would be to get reborn American and write their books in English.

Fortunately, they haven't yet done this.

One French writer who is extremely famous in English, though I know nothing about his sales, is the nineteenth-century novelist Gustave Flaubert. He is best-known for his treatise on boredom in the afternoon, *Madame Bovary*, but before I lived in France I had only read *The Sentimental Education*—or to be more accurate I had skimmed through it in translation. I took away little from that reading other than a confused panorama of French society in the mid-nineteenth century. In our first winter in the south, however, I decided to try reading it in French. This turned out to be an incredibly complex enterprise that stretched out over several weeks. Partly this was because I had to look up a lot of words—Flaubert is not the easiest writer—but also, having slowed down, I discovered the pleasure of reading Flaubert in this way. His sentences are meant to be carefully considered, to be read aloud, to be savoured slowly in the mouth like fine wine or rich food. He used to spend hours every night in his study writing, rewriting and reading aloud to make sure the sounds weren't "ugly." The idea that good writing can and must be as beautiful to the ear as great food is to the palate is one of the key ways in which French literature is totally different from English literature, and also explains why certain books one reads in French, while wildly popular there for the wonderful assonance of their vowel structures, make no sense in English. Flaubert was so proud of his sentences that he used to read his books aloud to his friends in long multi-hour sessions, about which they then wrote contemptuous comments in their diaries and letters.

Another element that slowed down my reading of the novel was its footnotes. There are about thirty pages of these notes, many of them dealing with Flaubert's reactions, or nonreactions, to comments on the manuscript by Maxime du Camp. I got completely caught up in why Flaubert had accepted or rejected the various suggestions.

By the time I finished I had an entirely new interpretation of this great book. It is the record of the corruption—and I mean this in almost the literal, physical sense of the word—of an innocent soul when exposed to the real world.

During our second winter in France, 1995–96, I read *The Sentimental Education* for the third time. This time my reading was informed by a curious four-page note by Marcel Proust about Flaubert's style. Flaubert, of course, was

Proust's great forerunner—Flaubert could be said to be the great forerunner of all the French fiction that followed him—and in his article Proust claimed that Flaubert's great revolution lay in his use of the imperfect tense, as opposed to the more literary past definite, which had previously been, and still is, considered the "correct" tense in which to write.

According to Proust, Flaubert used the imperfect rather than the past definite in order to change time from a series of discrete chunks, with beginnings and ends, into a flowing continuity. One of the great feats of *The Sentimental Education* is that it takes place over a long period of time yet is equally convincing at every point. And now, on this reading, I began to see that my previous interpretation of the novel had been only partial: yes, Flaubert was talking about corruption and change, but he was also saying that the complexities or compromises of the world didn't differ from purity and innocence only in the fact of their corruption; they also differed in that innocence stands outside time, whereas human lives are subject to its laws.

Portraying the changes in people and their relations over time was precisely the problem that had been paralyzing me with *Elizabeth and After*. It is far easier to set a novel within a limited framework of months or weeks, or even a few days (which is why thrillers happen fast). Now I knew what the problem was. I couldn't solve it by simply changing verb tenses, but I could at least think about it directly.

Another book I read with great care that winter was David Bronsen's biography of Joseph Roth. Roth (1894-1939) was a Jewish Austrian writer born in a tiny Polish town (then part of the Austro-Hungarian Empire) and moved as a young man first to Vienna, then to Munich, where he became precociously successful as a journalist, and began writing novels. During the 1920s he established a reputation as a gifted literary *flâneur*, though he considered himself a serious reporter and had great ambitions as a novelist—ambitions he soon fulfilled. In 1933, the day after Hitler came to power, he moved to Paris, which remained his base until his death in 1939. He is said to have drunk himself to death.

I was first introduced to Roth's books in 1986, when we were in Paris. His essay *Juifs en Errance*—a plea to readers to understand that Jews from Eastern Europe were so fundamentally and totally different in every respect from Westerners that they could not be judged by Western European standards—made a huge impression on me. It was a wonderfully observed statement about the true impossibility of bridging the abyss that separates the outsider from the mainstream. I began reading Roth's novels, then everything I could find about him.

I also became fascinated with Walter Benjamin, a German Jewish essayist and critic who ended up committing suicide in 1940 when, after making the arduous trek through the Franco-Spanish Pyrenees at the beginning of the Second World War, he was refused entrance to Spain. Like Roth, Benjamin worshipped France and, of course, Paris; one of his best-known essays is "Paris: Capital of the Nineteenth Century." For both men, as for so many other refugees, Paris was the capital not only of the nineteenth century but of *Europe*, that is to say, the centre of intellectual, ideological and racial freedom and tolerance, and the exact opposite of the dark nationalism espoused by Hitler and his allies. One of Benjamin's ambitions—and Benjamin was a man of impractical ambitions—was to live in Paris and be accepted by the French as a French critic, somehow supporting himself writing essays on French culture. However, his writing on French culture and literature had absolutely no impact on the French themselves: he was even less successful in becoming a French writer than he had been as a German one. His current fame and high intellectual standing—even the publication of most of his writings—came almost entirely after his death. Except to a few close friends, during his lifetime he was mostly unknown, usually impoverished and isolated.

Roth and Benjamin, like Franz Kafka, were writers who fascinated me because historical circumstances had made it impossible for them to have an anchoring culture. As Benjamin said about himself: "The goal I set for myself . . . is to be regarded as the foremost critic of German literature. The trouble is that for more than fifty years literary criticism in Germany has not been considered a serious genre. To create a place in criticism for oneself means to re-create it as a genre." Even had he begun to succeed by publishing one or more books, they would have been burned in 1933.

Like Kafka and Roth, Benjamin was in the double-bind common to all Western European Jews. On the one hand they could not entirely cast off their Jewishness and assimilate because they would always be seen as Jews. On the other hand they could not simply be Jews, because unless they wished to follow a (probably delusional) strategy of fanatic self-isolation, they would still have to live within a larger Christian environment.

As Kafka put it in a letter to Max Brod, the would-be German Jewish writer's despair was rooted in the absurdity of his situation, yet if he wrote about that despair his writing could not be a true part of German literature, because the problem was not a German but a Jewish one.

How familiar such complaints sound to a Canadian writer whose origin or sensibility lies outside the Canadian cultural mainstream. One of the strange things about being a writer in Canada—or at least, being this writer in Canada—is the gradual realization that if one is not writing books that represent the white, conservative, middle-class and Protestant values of the literary establishment, one is forever destined to be seen by that establishment, in terms of the recognition, rewards and prizes it has to offer, as unimportant and marginal—at best, a friendly mascot from another planet, to be accepted only if he is willing, in turn, to accept and serve the established order.

For anyone within that order, this statement of the case must seem very harsh, possibly even "ungrateful." But for those on the outside, I am sure it seems understated, underplayed to the point of trivializing the experience of writers on the margin, writers who gradually discover that the sociological impact of their books is bound to be limited, because they were born the wrong person or in the wrong place, or have a class interest other than the one that can be distilled from a careful reading of British Literature 100.

Of course, there would not be quite so many ignored books if books themselves, all books, weren't quite so ignored. And being on the literary margins isn't all that bad—it's a fine place from which to snipe and complain and explore the venial sins of greed, ambition, envy, lust, pride, etc., which are after all the golden lode of all great literature—except for Canadian literature, whose golden lode often appears to be the detailing of domestic life.

Oh dear, the offended critic will say, this really *is* getting offensive. There he goes again, that charming little fellow who has, after all, not gone unrewarded. Anyway, I thought he'd moved to France. Some people have all the luck.

And maybe they do. For example, as it turned out, Kafka was not a very accurate reader of his own situation: his books, the very ones he urged Brod to destroy without publishing, turned out to be literary classics. After his death.

When we got back to Canada from France in the summer of 1996, I had with me a new draft of *Elizabeth and After*. The manuscript was by now of elephantine proportions. I spent a few weeks trimming it down a bit and making a few cosmetic improvements. In October, after the publication of *Last Seen*, I set out on tour, leaving *Elizabeth* with my editor at Knopf, Diane Martin. This albatross was now ten years old. I had never shown it to anyone and what I needed most was to be relieved of the burden. As I explained to Diane (though probably she didn't need to be told), when I showed something to an editor what I usually wanted was enormous and excessive enthusiasm along with the offer of a contract. This time, however, I wanted something entirely different: I wanted to be told to put it away, possibly even burn it to ensure that I could never again take it out in a moment of weakness; and to think about something else. Doing something useful with my life. Finding a different book to write. Scratching out a teaching job somewhere. Anything.

Instead, perhaps just to be contrary, Diane read the manuscript and responded with enormous and excessive enthusiasm as well as the promise to try to get a contract.

"You're saying I should publish *this*?"

"No."

"You're saying I should work on it."

"Exactly."

"But I already have worked on it. That's the problem."

"And it has everything. All you need to do is pull it together. It won't take much."

"That's what I've been telling myself for years. And this is what I've got." Anyway, I knew what it meant when Diane said something wouldn't take much work. In this fashion she had gotten me to revise and rewrite *Last Seen* until the finished book had been pushed to a level far beyond that of the manuscript she had begun with. Yet seldom had she made any specific suggestion or criticism—her preferred tactic was to launch out with "I don't exactly understand why so-and-so does this . . ." or some other apparently innocuous request for clarification that would lead to the unravelling and reknitting of the entire book. For *Last Seen*, which had been a manuscript of two hundred pages, this had been possible. At more than twice that length, *Elizabeth and After* was like a giant ramshackle house just waiting to collapse.

She somehow talked me into it, and I spent most of the next two years rewriting and rewriting until the ramshackle house had (at least in my mind) turned into a polished intricate structure of which each component part was in balance with every other.

Elizabeth and After was obviously an inevitable point on the arc I'd seen so long ago when I began *The Disinherited*. If the Salem novels were a car, this new novel was the wall towards which they had been driving. In *The Disinherited*, the settling of the land, its literal shaping, the force of its presence, were the dominant factors in people's lives. Now, only twenty-five years later, there was a new reality, which was that this landscape was simply an ungroomed and half-exploited part of the giant suburb and hinterland of the dominant urban centres. The land had become mostly a museum, a memory, the repository of a mythology that few remembered, but that all were still influenced by.

Like *The Disinherited*, *Emotional Arithmetic* and *Last Seen*, *Elizabeth and After* was a book I found so difficult to write, I often worried I would die before finishing it. *The Disinherited* had overwhelmed me with sheer physical pain and resistance; *Emotional Arithmetic* had presented technical challenges it took years to resolve; with *Last Seen* I had a superstitious fear that like Daedalus, in order to get where I needed to go I was flying too close to the sun. *Elizabeth and After* presented itself as an unscaleable cliff. I knew this was a novel that couldn't work unless it was almost perfect. After each of the last few drafts of *Elizabeth and After* I would fall into an exhausted collapse, after which I would eat and exercise and indulge myself in unprecedented leisure until I felt fit enough to go back to it.

When it was finally done I decided I would reward myself with a trip to Paris. I hadn't been there for years and the opportunity had come up to sublet an apartment for a month. During this time, I thought, aside from wandering about and seeing old friends, I could visit the old Joseph Roth haunts and perhaps even do some research on this fascinating project that had the good manners to have no manuscript attached to it.

Another project on my mind was this memoir. I still had no idea how I would approach it, but the idea of wandering about Paris contemplating my completely meaningless life was appealing.

But as turned out to be the case with the story of the publication of *Emotional Arithmetic*, there is another layer in the history of this particular book.

One night in Paris, I went out to dinner with some friends. They suggested a restaurant in the Marais because it would be within walking distance of my sublet apartment, which was quite uniquely located in a building beside the Père Lachaise Cemetery, the permanent residence of such luminaries as Jim Morrison (his is the most visited grave), Abelard and Héloïse, Balzac, Colette and so many others that there is a vendor permanently stationed at the gates selling guides to the cemetery.

The restaurant, while attractively noisy and inexpensive, was so thick with cigarette smoke that the haze actually formed its own weather systems and cloud formations around each table. Choking and sick to our stomachs, we stumbled out after only a couple of hours and moved on to a nearby pool hall. It turned out to be almost as bad, but we stayed on drinking and playing until after midnight.

The next morning, the clothes I had worn smelled like a concentration of stuffed ashtrays, and even the chair on which I'd thrown them stank of raw French cigarettes. That afternoon I was still sick and called my friends to see how they were doing. They, too, were under the weather.

A few days later I spoke to them again. They had completely recovered from their restaurant-pool hall experience and were on to a bout of suspected food poisoning from a new bargain restaurant. I was still coughing away, and though I'd washed my clothes, twice, my lungs still felt as though they could use a trip to a desert to get cleaned out.

When I returned to Canada, *Elizabeth and After* was published. With a few exceptions, not, fortunately for me, in important places, it was better received critically than any of my previous books. A reprint was soon ordered and for the first time in a very long time I felt as though good fortune and luck had paid a visit to one of my books.

Meanwhile I still didn't feel right. It was as though—both physically and on other levels—something had gone dead inside me. I began going to the doctor. At first she said I had something called "the ninety-nine-day cough." This made sense. I'd been coughing for a while and didn't seem about to stop. But as time passed I didn't seem to be getting any better. Finally she took an X-ray and declared that I had pneumonia. When drugs had no effect there was a second X-ray and suddenly I was in the office of a hospital lung specialist, being given some very bad news. In fact, I'd been walking around incredibly ill for years, and the incident in the smoky restaurant and bar had merely triggered a set of symptoms that had been on the verge of manifesting. What I heard wasn't exactly unexpected—by now I had realized that something was terribly wrong—but it was certainly unwelcome.

One never knows, in such circumstances, how one will react. Looking back at my life I suppose my response was to be expected, but at the time I was surprised to find myself being so decisive. In any case, after telling the children, who along with Patsy and a few close friends have, through their ferocious loyalty and love, fashioned me a protective cloak that has made the impossible bearable, the first thing I did was to vow to myself that come what may I was going to finish three more books: a book of short stories that had been contracted along with *Elizabeth* and needed only two more stories to be complete, this memoir and the Joseph Roth novel. I spoke to my publishers about it and they reacted with enormous speed and generosity.

The story book is now in proofs. This memoir is almost complete. As for the Roth novel, I've reached the stage of having gone too far to turn back, yet still can't imagine exactly where I'll end up or how I'll ever finish. This is my favourite part of a novel—the slow and always surprising discovery of its particular universe, with its language, its people, its cities and countryside. For the next several years, I'll be inhabiting these people and this place, waiting for their secrets to be revealed. For me it is the very essence of writing, and what has made the writing life the only one I could live.

The Works of Matt Cohen

Korsoniloff (House of Anansi Press, 1969)
Johnny Crackle Sings (McClelland & Stewart, 1971)
Columbus and the Fat Lady (House of Anansi Press, 1972)
Too Bad Galahad (Coach House Press, 1972)
The Disinherited (McClelland & Stewart, 1974)
Peach Melba (Coach House Press, 1973)
Wooden Hunters (McClelland & Stewart, 1975)
The Colours of War (McClelland & Stewart, 1977)
Night Flights (Doubleday, 1978)
The Leaves of Louise (McClelland & Stewart, 1978)
The Sweet Second Summer of Kitty Malone (McClelland & Stewart, 1979)
Flowers of Darkness (McClelland & Stewart, 1981)
The Expatriate (General, 1982)
Café Le Dog (McClelland & Stewart, 1983)
The Spanish Doctor (McClelland & Stewart, 1984)
In Search of Leonardo (Coach House Press, 1985)
Nadine (Viking, 1986)
Living On Water (Viking, 1986)
Emotional Arithmetic (Lester & Orpen Dennys, 1990)
Freud: The Paris Notebooks (Quarry Press, 1990-91)
The Bookseller (Knopf Canada, 1993)
Lives of the Mind Slaves (The Porcupine's Quill, 1994)
Last Seen (Knopf Canada, 1996)
Elizabeth and After (Knopf Canada, 1999)
Getting Lucky (posthumous, Knopf Canada, 2000)

INDEX

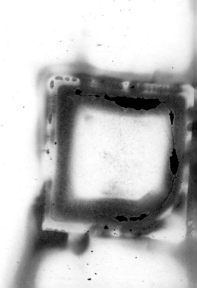